Table Of Co

PART 1

PART 2

DEDICATION

This book is first dedicated to God The Father, God The Son and God The Holy Spirit. I am grateful to my Heavenly Father for calling me into His marvellous Light, I am thankful to Jesus Christ for prevailing at the garden of Gethsemane and I thank the Holy Spirit for being so patient with me.

I am thankful to my parents for being the vehicles that brought me into this world, for loving me, caring for me and providing for me. I am very thankful to all my brothers and sisters - thanks for your love and support.

I am thankful to Christ Love Fellowship at Obafemi Awolowo University, Nigeria, for being the Church that led me to Christ. I am grateful for allowing me to serve at the Watchtower department - where I was taught how to pray and hear the voice of God. I am grateful to the watchtower members and especially to Pastor Kayode.

I am grateful to my Cell members in Kensington Temple Church, London. I am grateful to the Kensington temple Church in Slough, UK, and to Pastor Camila - thank you for allowing me to serve in the Church of the Lord. I am very grateful to the Church of Victorious Pentecostal Assembly in Barking, Essex, UK and to Pastor Alex and Patricia Omokudu, for their commitment to the work of the Lord - thank you for teaching the body of Christ how to manifest the glory of God on the Earth.

I am grateful to Mr and Mrs Adebisi of Marella International College, Ibadan, Oyo state, Nigeria for their love and support. I am grateful to Miss Folake Olatunji, my friend, my encourager, my helper, my sister and hopefully my wife - I am very grateful to you for your love and encouragement.

Books cannot contain the names of all the people that I owe an appreciation to, but may God reward every man according to his work. Thanks to Tony, Saira etc

Thanks to you all.

Mr Oladapo Ashiru (The Author).

INTRODUCTION

In the beginning, the idea of writing a book was too hard for me to accept, but with God, all things are truly possible. It started on the 31st of January, 2010, when I woke up around 7am and realized that the Holy Spirit had been ministering some truth analogies to me which I have hereby documented. The revelations and insights spanned over a period of about 30 months from that beautiful morning, and to God be the glory Who began and also finished His work, Amen.

It is the similarities that the Holy Spirit showed me concerning the faith walk of a believer to the vehicles that we drive. I pray that The Holy Spirit being the perfect teacher would paint the picture with the greatest clarity in the mind of every reader, Amen.

When we study in schools, we are usually presented with images that make what is being taught to be easier to visualize and understand. It is easy for people to remember things when they see them. Better still, it is easier for people to remember things when they both see and hear them. It is even much better when they see, hear and do them. When we do something over a period of time, it simply becomes part of us.

This is actually a biblical concept. Do not be hearers only but doers of the Word. May God make us doers of His word and not just hearers only. As the bible says, faith comes by hearing and hearing by the word of God, but faith without works is dead. Therefore, after hearing the word of God, the next step is to do it in order to see results in our lives. I call it the application of the word!

Therefore, this book was inspired to trigger a reminder in the mind of every believer about their "level of doing the word of God", every time we see a vehicle or better still, every time we drive one. Immaturity is a serious issue in the body of Christ and I pray that the Lord would open our eyes of understanding to see the reason(s) why this is so and what we need to do in order to become mature believers, even to the stature of Christ Himself. Amen.

Thank you for reading.
Oladapo Ashiru.

Your New Life
VS
Your Old Life

1 Thessalonians 5:23 says:
"Now may the God of peace Himself sanctify you completely; and may your whole spirit, soul and body be preserved blameless at the coming of our Lord Jesus Christ."

The scripture above is from a letter that apostle Paul wrote to some Christians in Thessalonian. These were believers because they were already born-again at this time. They have been born of the word of God by the Holy Spirit and they are now spiritually connected to God!

Whether a man is born-again or not, he is a spirit, he has a soul and he lives in a body. Man is not just his "mere" body! His body is just merely part of him. He is a spirit that lives inside his body. To depart from one's body is to die physically, but a man's spirit lives on. When someone becomes born-again, their spirit which was disconnected from God is now recreated with the ability to connect to God permanently through the Holy Spirit who now lives in them.

Notice that before you became a born-again believer, you could not worship God in the spirit because your spirit was disconnected from God but now, your spirit has been recreated to connect to God in the spirit. God can now release some fire on you in the spirit. Now, when you worship God you raise up your hands, you dance, you sing, you leap with joy - you worship Him with your spirit in the spirit.

Romans 8:14 says:
"As many as are led by the Spirit of God, they are called sons of God".

Notice that the scripture did not say "Sons and daughters"! Whether you are a man or woman, once you become born-again, you become a child of God that matures into a son of God. Let us not be fleshly-minded, "son of God" is not talking about gender but rather, "position, authority, power, royalty e t c". A son of God is a son of God either he is male or she is female.

Are you born-again? If yes, then, you are no more limited to the resources of the physical, but you can now tap into the spiritual realm! You can now function as a spirit, you now have powers that you never had before, you can now do things that are totally impossible for an unbeliever to do or imagine etc. Can an unbeliever raise the dead and cast out demons or speak to the mountains to move?

In fact the scripture below makes it clear that a new law applies to you now!

Romans 8:2 says:
"The law of the spirit of life in Christ Jesus has set me free from the law of sin and death".

The scripture is saying that you used to sin and you had no power not to sin, because you were under the law of sin and death. But now that you are born-again, you operate under the law of the spirit of life and because of this, sin no more has power over you and you now have the power to sin no more! You now have a power that you never had before you became born-again!! HALLELUYAH!!!

In our vehicle analogy, your body is like the body of a vehicle and your spirit is like the engine of a vehicle. Your soul consists of your will, emotions, feelings, mind e t c but the mind has a central influence over your soul and therefore, I would be referring to your soul as your mind. Your mind is like the driver of a vehicle. As your mind controls what you do in life, so does the driver of a vehicle, control what the vehicle does or where it goes. The vehicle is like your life or ministry. The passengers are the people that you are assigned to influence. To a pastor, the passengers are the people in his church. To a married man, the passengers are his family.

Therefore, when you became born-again, your body did not change. Your body size, color, shape e t c remained the same. Your soul or mind did not change, but you got a new spirit which is like a new engine of a vehicle. Therefore, you can now do things that you could never do before. Therefore, when God says to you in the bible, you are healed or rich or anointed or redeemed e t c, He is talking to you based on your new identity in the spirit.

The following illustration should help clarify this. Imagine if you have a cart with four wheels. You pull this cart about with ropes to wherever you are going. It would take a lot of hassle and sweat to go about in life like this every day. Now, if you attach the ropes of the cart to two horses, suddenly, it gets much easier and faster to get things done. All you have to do now is work with the two horses to drive your cart. But, how much better does it get, if your cart can be totally renewed and fitted with a 100 horse-power car engine with gears, steering, lights, battery, sound system, air conditioning e t c !

The explanation of the analogy here is; the man that pulls his cart with ropes around is the normal natural unbeliever who has no power of God in his life to help him pull the loads of his life. He pulls, he sweats, he buys, he sells, he does it all by himself without allowing God to help him lighten the burden of his life. That is the example of a man who is not yet born-again. He cannot tap into the power of God from without or within. This is wisdom – some unbelievers have allowed demonic powers to push their cart for them hence, they do evil and seem to prosper! Their prosperity surely never lasts or endures. No wonder they are rich one day and the next day, they are broke or depressed or addicted! Only the blessing of the Lord makes a man rich and adds no sorrow to it. Brothers and sisters, the blessing from the devil always add sorrows.

The man that has two horses attached to his cart is an example of the old-testament people who were anointed by the anointing oil or the Holy Spirit e.g. High-priests, prophets and kings etc. These were anointed by God for different purposes. The anointing on them was an empowerment that multiplied their efforts. They had the anointing of the Holy Spirit on the outside like a cloth that is worn, which helped them to do things that they could not do by their own power alone. The Holy Spirit could not live inside them because they still had the sinful nature of the first Adam. Therefore, the Holy Spirit only clothed them from the outside. They had access to the power of God from the outside.

The man with the 100 horse-power car engine cart which we

can also represent as a modern day vehicle, is an example of a born-again believer who has the Holy Spirit inside him and with him. These ones are totally new creatures that never existed before, with powers that are yet to be realized, and so are you, if you are born-again. Yet, they look like the same old cart from the outside-physically, but from the inside-spiritually, they are totally new, different and far more powerful than before.

2 Corinthians 5:17 says:
"Therefore, if anyone is in Christ, he is a new creation; old things have passed away; behold, all things have become new".

As born-again believers with such powerful and sophisticated machinery at our disposal, we need to be taught how to use such powers properly because if we are not taught, we would continue to pull our carts with ropes when we can be travelling at miles per hour with no sweat whatsoever!

As a born-again believer, the bible is the book that educates us about what God has placed inside of us when we became born-again. In order for our new machine or vehicle to deliver what it is designed to do, we, the driver of that vehicle, needs to be re-educated. Therefore, in order for a born-again Christian to mature and do what God says they can do, the mind of that believer needs to be re-educated or renewed.

Romans 12:2
"Do not be conformed to this world, but be transformed by the re-newing of your mind..."

If the driver of the combustion-engine cart does not know that the cart is now much more powerful than it used to be, he would end up doing things the way he used to and keep on getting the same old poor results!

Many believers are like this. They are already born-again, they have a new car engine in their cart, but because they don't know much about their new identity, they are still pulling the cart by the ropes, gasping under the loads of life e t c when they should be travelling through life at ease.

Some other believers know that they are now spiritual empowered, but instead of spending time to learn more about how to live their lives in the spirit and by the Holy Spirit, they assume that their new identities cannot really do them much good than merely taking them to heaven, and so, they are not keen to investing quality time in the things of God. Also, since most were taught that becoming born-again is all about going to heaven, and since they are already born-again as a form of insurance policy to get to heaven, they see no reason why they should devote quality time to seek the kingdom of God and His righteousness e t c?

A believer might ask, what is the purpose of giving my precious time into the things of God? Dear reader, the purpose has everything to do with your present life and the life after this age!

The rewards of attaining maturity as a believer is what I strongly believe Jesus Christ is talking about in the letter to the seven churches in the book of revelation when He continually says "To him that overcomes.... " ? He that overcomes is the one who devoted time and effort into the things of God in order to attain maturity.

On the other hand, the rewards of attaining maturity as a believer in this life are reflected in the personal life of Jesus

Christ on this earth. He prospered without sweating. Instead of circumstances controlling Him, He controlled circumstances. But more importantly, the way He lived His life made people desire to want to know God. Will it not be so sweet if people can just look at our lives and beg us to introduce them to our God! When they see our joy, love, health, wealth, wisdom, understanding, peace e t c then we are surely witnessing and preaching the gospel. The gospel is being down-graded to mere talking when it should be more of bearing witness with our lives. We should not just talk the talk but walk the talk.

May we desire spiritual maturity if not for our own sake, then at least for the sake of the kingdom of God. As painful as it may sound, some unbelievers might never make it to heaven because the believers around them only testified with their mouths but not with their lives. Actions they say, speak louder than words.

When some believers are supposed to be spending time in the things of the Word - Bible, books, church, DVD, conferences, praying, fasting e t c in order to learn more about their new identity, they are spending time on the things of the world - wild-partying, gossiping, corrupt communication, lustful or violent entertainment, negative news, rebellion, wrath, drunkenness, fornication, adultery, sexual perversion, gluttony, idolatry, pursuing riches, pursuing pleasures of the flesh etc

Some may argue that the author doesn't seem to understand that sin is pleasurable. I reply by saying: "God created us to take pleasure in anything that we choose. But, the greatest pleasure is truly in the presence of God".

Psalm 16:11

You make known to me the path of life; in your presence there is fullness of joy; at your right hand are pleasures forevermore.

If a man can spend all his life on the things of the world, it makes sense to say that another man can easily spend all his life on the things of God. I personally hope to get to the place where, only the things of God remain in my life, so that the Lord can increase while I decrease.

Finally, using the car engine cart as an example, in order to get this cart to do what it is designed to do, we need to learn how the various parts function e.g. engine, navigation system, sound system, gears, steering, pedals, lights e t c This means that as a born-again believer, in order to function properly as spiritual beings, we need to learn about the many things that we have been given e.g. faith, prayer, bible, worship, praise, faith friends, church, Holy Spirit etc.

This is what we shall be addressing henceforth. We shall be talking about your spirit compared to the engine of your vehicle, your body compared to the body of your vehicle, your mind compared to you-the driver of the vehicle e t c

The driver of a vehicle plays a very crucial role in the lifespan of a vehicle. If the driver believes that driving the vehicle roughly is nice, the vehicle would hardly last long. One driver decides that servicing his vehicle is very unnecessary and he ends up with a big bill for repairs. Another driver decides to regularly service his vehicle and he saves himself a lot of troubles. In essence, your mind determines the path that you go through in life and ultimately where you end up in life.

Your mind is simply where you process thoughts into words and actions. In essence, your mind actually has no problem, it is the thoughts that you allow into your mind that is the main issue. The main difference in people is not their color or race but their way of thinking.

Proverbs 23:7
As a man thinks, so is he.

It is illegal in most countries to drive a vehicle while drunk. This is not just dangerous to the driver and the passengers, but very dangerous to the other road users.

Many believers are still running their lives through a "drunken mindset" or "carnal mind" or for lack of words "pulling-the-cart-by-the-rope mentality". As it was said earlier, your body is like the body of a vehicle, your spirit is like the engine of a vehicle and your mind is like the driver of a vehicle. Living life through a "drunken-mindset" is like allowing a drunk driver to take you from one destination to another. To make it really simple,

That mindset can kill you!

Which one of us would ever board a vehicle if we obviously see that the driver is acting drunk? We would never board such a vehicle. Yet, most of us perhaps unknowingly, run our lives this way!

A "drunken-mindset" or "carnal mind" or "pulling-the-cart-by-the-rope mindset" is a mindset that says the opposite of what God says. The carnal-mind leads to death. The opposite of the carnal mind is a spiritual mind or to be spiritually-minded.

A spiritual mind agrees with what God says while a carnal mind disagrees with what God says. In essence, you might be spiritually minded in your sexual life, but when it comes to your finances, you might be carnally minded.

For example, God says fornication or sex before marriage is wrong and if you agree with that scripture, you are spiritually minded in that area of your life and you will experience the power of God in that area of your life. Now, God says give your offerings and tithes, and if you disagree with that scripture, you are carnally-minded in that area of your life and the power of God would not be able to manifest in your finances.

Please let us take a quick look at a scripture again.

1 Thessalonians 5:23 says:
"Now may the God of peace Himself sanctify you completely; and may your whole spirit, soul and body be preserved blameless at the coming of our Lord Jesus Christ."

Your spirit is already righteous, redeemed, saved, born-again, born of God.

Your Soul or Mind needs to be purified or sanctified by the word of God. You have to actively work with God to get this done.

Your body is neutral. When Jesus comes, our body will transform to His glorious body.

The scripture above says that may the God of peace Himself sanctify you **completely**. The walk of a believer into maturity is a process of different stages. It takes time to mature. God Himself wants to sanctify you or purify you completely. In order to sanctify you completely, your soul or mind needs to be totally renewed. Your mind can only be renewed at your will, not by your power. You provide the will, God provides the power. Some people think that will-power can help them renew their mind and ways. When they realize that they are in a spiritual battle, they would trash their willpower and humbly ask God for the power of deliverance. You can never cleanse your mind by your own willpower. Only the word of God has the power to purify your mind!

Philippians 2:5
"Let this mind be in you, which was also in Christ Jesus.

Jesus Christ always agrees and does what God says and so, He is totally spiritually minded. Therefore, the power of God is evident in His life. Jesus Christ said "I only say what my Father says, and I only do what my Father does."

1 John 5:7
For there are three that bear record in heaven, the Father, the Word, and the Holy Spirit: and these three are one.

We have God in Heaven who hears our prayers.
We have The Word of God to show us how God thinks.
We have the Holy Spirit Who teaches us all things.

Therefore brothers and sisters, we have no reason not to be spiritually minded just like Jesus Christ was spiritually minded!

We have God in heaven who hears our prayers.
Matthew 6:8:
Our Father Who hath in heaven.

We have the Word of God- Bible, to show us how God thinks.
Jeremiah 29:11
For I know the thoughts that I think towards you, says the Lord, thoughts of peace and not of evil, to give you a future and a hope.

We have the Holy Spirit of God who teaches us all things.
John 14:26
But the Helper, the Holy Spirit, whom the Father will send in My Name, He will teach you all things....

Again, what happens when you become spirit-minded in all the areas of your life? You become a mature believer. The power of God is greatly accessible by you. Demons and circumstances bow before you. Just read about the life of Jesus to see what it means to be mature. It is a place of dominion over sin, lack, disease, sickness, poverty etc. It is the place of power and authority. It is the place where nothing is impossible. It is the place of great faith which moves great mountains.

Imagine Jesus feeding more than 5,000 people with five loaves and two fish. He did not file for bankruptcy, He did not apply for a loan, He simply asked that the people sit down in groups of fifties, and then, having so much confidence in Jehovah-The Provider, He thanked God, blessed, broke the food. Then He gave His disciples the food to distribute and the people ate so much that even 12 baskets remained!

Do you know that we do the same thing but in a different way?

When sometimes we have no food at home or we don't feel like cooking, we pick up the phone and call a food delivery service.

Perhaps we pay them in advance on the phone and thank them in advance for the food we have not yet seen. Then we ask our family members and friends to prepare to eat, set the plates on the table while someone is perhaps grumbling for the lateness of the arrival of the food. Finally, the doorbell rings, and there it is, we have the food delivered!

Jesus Christ spiritually phoned the shop of God in prayer, used His faith to make an order of some loaves of bread and fish, thanked the Father, asked the people to prepare to eat, and just in time, the delivery was made !

People of God, let us learn how to order from the shop of God by being spirit-minded. In this shop of God, there is always more than enough and all we need to make orders is our faith!

Philippians 4:19
My God shall supply all your needs according to His Riches in Glory by Christ Jesus.

Come on Brothers and Sisters, let us all become spiritually-minded as our Father wants us to be. Let everyone check the driver behind the vehicle of their lives. Does that driver/mind agree with what God says in every area of our lives? God has power available to us to renew our mind but we have to be willing by studying and doing the word of God.

Romans 8:6
To be spiritually-minded is life and peace.

Matthew 5:8

Blessed are the pure at heart, for they shall see God.

Romans 8:14

As many as are led by the Holy-Spirit, these are sons of God.

Your Body
VS
Vehicle Body

Genesis 1:26

"And God said: Let us create man in Our image, according to our likeness."

Of course, every one of us knows that people come in different body sizes, colors and shapes etc. It is even more interesting that every man has a different fingerprint compared to every other man on the earth!

Vehicles also come in different shapes and colors and for different purposes. A truck is designed and manufactured to carry heavy loads e.g. for delivery services. A sports car is created to carry people with their small loads or perhaps for racing! Don't use your sports car for a delivery service, and don't use your truck for racing.

God has created every man for different purposes. Every man is totally distinct from the other. God created you the way you are and you are the best the way you look, and there can never be a better looking you. You are the best you, that can ever be!

Don't compete with yourself! You cannot win yourself!

1 Corinthians 6:19
Or do you not know that your body is a temple of the Holy Spirit Who is in you, Whom you have from God, ... ?

Your body is where the spirit of God dwells. When you become a born-again, the spirit of God comes to live inside of you.

With most of us, if the president of our country decides to move in with us for a week, significant changes would be noticed by our neighbors. All of a sudden, the grass in the garden is now well-trimmed, looking lush-green; the house is re-painted, the furniture is changed or polished etc. Sure, we might not be able to afford all that we want done, but we would do the best with all we've got. In fact, some people would not mind getting in debt to re-furbish the house in order to make a good impression. So also, since the God of the universe has moved in with us, in our body, we ought to take care of our body. We ought to eat right, dress right, exercise right, sleep right etc. We ought to carry ourselves with confidence as the carriers of the presence of God or as the carriers of the ark of covenant, knowing fully well that no un-authorized individual can mess with us without experiencing the wrath of God. Something actually happened in the bible that illustrated this.

2 Samuel 6:7
"And the anger of the LORD was kindled against Uzzah, and God struck him down there because of his error, and he died there beside the ark of God."

In the passage above, Uzzah touched the ark of covenant, which was like the house that carried God's presence in the Old Testament, but he was not authorized to touch it and guess what happened, he died. Maturity as a believer is realizing that if sickness touches our body, it must die. But until we mature to see this, sickness, diseases etc would usually rule our bodies!

Someone demonstrated this maturity in the Old Testament in the name of Prophet Elisha. Elisha knew Whom He carried and in fact, the popular biblical statement that goes thus: "They that are with us are more than they that are with them" was framed through his mouth. Let's have a quick look into what happened.

2 Kings 6:8-18
Now the king of Aram was at war with Israel. After conferring with his officers, he said, "I will set up my camp in such and such a place." The man of God sent word to the king of Israel: "Beware of passing that place, because the Arameans are going down there." So the king of Israel checked on the place indicated by the man of God. Time and again Elisha warned the king, so that he was on his guard in such places.

This enraged the king of Aram. He summoned his officers and demanded of them, "Tell me! Which of us is on the side of the king of Israel?" "None of us, my lord the king," said one of his officers, "but Elisha, the prophet who is in Israel, tells the king of Israel the very words you speak in your bedroom." "Go, find out where he is," the king ordered, "so I can send men and capture him." The report came back: "He is in Dothan." Then he sent horses and chariots and a strong force there. They went by night and surrounded the city.

When the servant of the man of God got up and went out early the next morning, an army with horses and chariots had surrounded the city. "Oh no, my lord! What shall we do?" the servant asked. "Don't be afraid," the prophet answered. "Those

who are with us are more than those who are with them." And Elisha prayed, "Open his eyes, LORD, so that he may see." Then the LORD opened the servant's eyes, and he looked and saw the hills full of horses and chariots of fire all around Elisha.
As the enemy came down toward him, Elisha prayed to the LORD, "Strike this army with blindness." So he struck them with blindness, as Elisha had asked.

Imagine if believers would laugh at thieves that point guns at their face, because they know that all they have to do is simply speak the word only, and the angel of the Lord would seize the gun, arrest the culprit and subdue them to the floor for the police to finish the job. Crimes would simply drop to zero because the criminals would not want to harass anyone anymore because they would argue, "What if the person is a Christian"? That would usher in the biggest salvation of souls in history!

As many vehicles these days are fitted with CCTV cameras to record what is happening around the vehicle, in order to deter crimes, we should realize that the Lord has his eyes on us and He also has his angels around us, watching everything that is happening and is about to happen around us !

Psalms 34:7
"The angel of the LORD encamps around those who fear him, and delivers them."

We should also realize that the same way that alarm systems are fitted into vehicles, so that when an un-authorized person tries to steal something from such vehicles, the alarm is triggered - we are also wired with the alarm system of the Holy Spirit who lives within us, Who alarms us of dangers and how to prevent them.

Zechariah 2:8
"For thus said the LORD of hosts, after his glory sent me to the nations who plundered you, for he who touches you touches the apple of his eye."

Dear reader, also recognize that no one can touch the apple of God's eye and goes without being punished! Neither Pharaohs of bondages nor Goliaths of oppression e t c touched God's people without receiving the judgment of death. You shall surely live and not die.

Your Spirit
VS
Vehicle Engine

Ephesians 4:4
There is One Body and One Spirit.

You are a spirit, you have a soul and you live in your body. The engine of your vehicle is like your spirit. When the bible talks about your heart, it is not talking about your blood-pumping organ, it is talking about your spiritual heart. It's referring to your heart in your spirit, not the heart in your body.

When you become born-again, your spirit is changed to a new spirit that is born of God, having the attributes of God in it.

2 Corinthians 5:17

Therefore if anyone is in Christ, he is a new creature; the old things passed away; behold, new things have come.

When God says, you are redeemed, you are saved, you have power over sin, you are born of God, you are more than a conqueror, you can do all things through Christ which strengthens you e t c He is talking about your new spirit, because remember, the real you is your spirit, you only live in your body. We don't really see our true selves, we only see our body. Actually, I have seen my spirit before in a dream. I looked exactly like my body but rather than being made of flesh, I am made of light. Predominantly around my face was a radiance of light shining forth. It is really glorious, I mean, I just remember saying to another friend in the dream "Look at me! Look at me! Look at my face"! Your true self is your spirit, and in order to see your spirit, you need to see the image of your spirit and since you were created in the image of God, it is important to look at God through the bible in order to see yourself. The more you know about God, the more you know about your real self.

John 4:24
God is Spirit and those who worship Him must worship Him in spirit and in truth.

Because you are born of God, you are like Him, a spirit.
Psalms 82:6
"I said 'You are gods' ".

The word of God- Bible is spirit.
John 6:63
The words that I speak to you, they are spirit and they are life.

Inside your spirit is where the power of God resides. In order to experience the power of God, you need to allow the power of God to flow from your spirit through your soul/mind to your body and then to the outside.

Just like in a vehicle, you need to allow the engine of a vehicle to release power through the driver of the vehicle, to the wheels of the vehicle and then the action is seen on the outside.

But, can the engine of a vehicle release power if there is no fuel in the vehicle? Sure, fuel must be available and that fuel is the word of God, which is the bible, but we would talk about that later on a deeper level.

When you fill your vehicle with fuel, the fuel only has the potential to provide energy. It must be channeled into the right system to provide power. The fuel enters the combustion engine, where a spark plug ignites fire to the fuel to release heat energy, which is converted to mechanical energy, which is used to move the wheels of the vehicle.

The spark plug in your engine is like a function of the Spirit of God. The Holy Spirit provides fire on the fuel-word of God. When you meditate on the word of God, you are allowing the Holy Spirit to provide fire to the fuel-the word of God.

AS THE POWER IN THE DIESEL OR PETROL IS RELEASED TO THE VEHICLE THROUGH THE BURNING OF THE FUEL IN THE ENGINE, SO ALSO, THE POWER IN THE WORD OF GOD IS RELEASED BY BURNING THE WORD OF GOD WITH THE FIRE OF THE HOLY-SPIRIT THROUGH THE MEDITATION OF THE WORD.

Some people read the bible but because they do not have the Holy Spirit in their life, the word of God delivers no power in their lives. It is like fueling your vehicle but the spark-plug in your engine is faulty. No power is released and your vehicle simply stops functioning. This does not mean that the fuel in your vehicle lacks power, it is simply an issue of absence of fire.

There are some religious groups in this category who notice the lack of power in their lives and instead of humbly asking God for the reason why this is so, they assume that the Holy Spirit must have retired back to heaven after the last apostles.

Most of these people would fuel their vehicles and surely except power to be released by their vehicles. If power is not released by their vehicles, they know there is a problem and they are quick to call for help from mechanics or vehicle repairers. Yet, they fill themselves with the word of God, they see no power and they do not ask questions as to what could be wrong.

Don't just be hearers of the word but doers least you deceive yourselves. The bible is a book of signs, wonders and miracles and when you hear the word of God and do it, you must experience signs, wonders and miracles yourself. Anything short of this means, there is a fault or lie or deception somewhere e.g. deception of sin, doctrines of men, traditions, deception of pleasure or riches choking the word e t c May the Lord fish every deception out of our lives in Jesus Name, Amen.

You observe many "so called churches" today and you hear their word without the power. What is wrong? As Gideon asked, where are the miracles that our Fathers told us about? Where are the mighty miracles of how they were saved by a mighty hand, from the hands of the Egyptians?

These days, we see "so called" church buildings turning to houses, clubs and pubs e t c because there is no power! John the Baptist did not scream with a loud-speaker to get people to listen to him! The fire of the Holy Spirit released so much power that people were astonished at his words. When Jesus came in the Power of the Holy Ghost after being led by the navigator system of the Holy Spirit, He did not scream for people to follow

Him, He did not entice them with fancy words or say things that they love to hear so that they would come to Him! He did not invite them to come and have coffee and tea with biscuits! He simply released the Power of the Word of God by the Holy Spirit.

The world looks desolate with problems from disease, poverty, famine, homelessness, injustice e t c People don't want someone just telling them that Jesus loves them when they are in pain and in hopelessness. People want to see the love and power of God in action. The world needs men and women of God to rise up, people who would walk in power, authority, love etc. People who would fulfill the prophecy of Jesus saying:

John 14:12
"Most assuredly, I say to you, he who believes in Me, the works that I do he will do also; and greater works than these he will do, because I go to My Father."

Jesus healed the sick, He fed the hungry, He raised the dead, He cast out demons and evil spirits trembled and begged for mercy in His Presence e t c

Yet, diseases thrive in some of today's churches, poverty stinks in the congregation, demons attend many churches these days without any fear or intimidation, in fact, instead of evil spirits begging for mercy, they seem to be taking over some pulpits!

Dear reader, I believe that you are not like this. You have been saved. You have been redeemed. You love your Father, you love Jesus, You fellowship with the Holy Spirit, you read and meditate on the word, and soon enough:

GOD WILL RELEASE HIS POWER TO YOU AND THROUGH YOU!

Proverbs 4:23
Keep your heart with all diligence, for out of it spring the issues of life.

What is this scripture saying? It is saying, guard what you are being taught. Re-evaluate the doctrines that you are being taught in your church! Take heed what you hear. Be careful of the kind of information that you allow into you, into your heart, into your spirit because, as a man thinks, so is he.

We are aware that if a vehicle is filled with the wrong type of fuel, the engine would knock. In fact, a knocked engine is hardly repairable and you usually have to replace the engine. Once you are born-again, the devil would TRY AS MUCH AS POSSIBLE to intoxicate you with wrong doctrines.

He would flood you with words from the newspapers, media, movies, music, daily news, friends, enemies e t c . The devil is cunny and very deceptive in his dealings. He would hold before you a keg that says petrol, but after careful analysis, it is probably 85% petrol and 15% water. He knows that if he asks you to fill up your vehicle with 100% water, you would say NO, therefore he would capitalize on your ignorance of the WORD to rob you.

Therefore, once the devil knows that you are not willing to live without the word of God, he would send out false preachers who preach the diluted word of God. Remember, false preachers preach the word, only that it is diluted or twisted. That adulteration is usually undetected by immature believers and that is another reason why their lives bear no fruits.

Many of us know that whether a drink is 1% alcoholic or 100% alcoholic, they will both get you drunk, it is just a matter of time. Therefore, it is important that a believer gets acquainted with the word of God, consistently every day.

Matthew 6:11
Give us this day our daily bread.

Please let us briefly analyze a situation in the bible.

The devil was tempting Jesus Christ and he said to Jesus:

"If you are the Son of God, throw yourself down?" (UNBIBLICAL)
Then, the devil covered the dilution by quoting the bible directly:

"He shall give His angels charge over you, In their hands they shall bear you up, lest you dash your foot against a stone". (BIBLICAL)

But, the full scripture goes below:

Psalm 91:9-12
"Because you have made the Lord, who is my refuge, even the Most High, your dwelling place, no evil shall be-fall you nor shall any plague come near your dwelling. For He shall give His Angels charge over you, to keep you in all your ways"

In essence, the devil twisted the scripture to try to put doubt in the heart of Jesus, by suggesting that Jesus should fall down and see if God would truly fulfill His promise of protection.

THE DEVIL IS SIMPLY TRYING TO ROB YOU OF YOUR FAITH, AND HE KNOWS THAT YOU GET FAITH THROUGH HEARING THE TRUE WORD OF GOD, THEREFORE, WHEN HE SEES THAT YOU ARE THE TYPE THAT IS CONSISTENTLY TRYING TO FEED ON THE WORD OF GOD, THE DEVIL WOULD TRY TO FEED YOU WITH WORDS THAT CONTRADICT THE WORD OF GOD, IF YOU MAKE YOURSELF ACCESSIBLE TO THEM.

Therefore, I say to you again, be very careful about what you hear, about the kind of information that you are open to. Be open-minded but be totally close-hearted. Filter information by the word of God in your mind, and if it agrees with the word of God, allow it to stay in your mind long enough and it will enter your heart or spirit or engine.

But if any information, word from a doctor, banker, friend, enemy e t c contradicts what the word of God says, reject that word, rebuke it, replace it with the word of God and faith would be released from that word, and you would live a victorious life because we overcome the world through faith.

Philippians 4:8

Finally, brothers, whatever is true, whatever is noble, whatever is right, whatever is pure, whatever is lovely, whatever is admirable—if anything is excellent or praiseworthy—think about such things.

Your Mind
VS
Vehicle Driver

Romans 12:2

Do not conform any longer to the pattern of this world, but be transformed by the renewing of your mind. Then you will be able to test and approve what God's will is—his good, pleasing and perfect will.

Like a car taken to a car wash for a clean-up, many Christians try to clean-up their body or "outside" in order to look holy and blessed, rather than cleaning up their mind or "inside" in order to be holy and be blessed !

When the inside is in the light, the outside will just be right. As it is written, by their fruits you shall know them.

Perhaps, we should have a quick look at the parable of the sower.

Mark 4:14-20

The sower soweth the word. And these are they by the way side, where the word is sown; but when they have heard, Satan cometh immediately, and taketh away the word that was sown in their hearts.

And these are they likewise which are sown on stony ground; who, when they have heard the word, immediately receive it with gladness; And have no root in themselves, and so endure but for a time: afterward, when affliction or persecution ariseth for the word's sake, immediately they are offended.

And these are they which are sown among thorns; such as hear the word, And the cares of this world, and the deceitfulness of riches, and the lusts of other things entering in, choke the word, and it becometh unfruitful.

And these are they which are sown on good ground; such as hear the word, and receive it, and bring forth fruit, some thirtyfold, some sixty, and some an hundred.

This parable indicates four kinds of people and the revelation that I have about these people is as follows:

(1) **They by the way side:** These are unbelievers who hear the word but it makes no sense to them and since they are still under the influence of the devil, the devil himself takes away the word that was sown in their hearts.

Some people who go to church actually belong to this category. They have no relationship with Jesus, they are not yet saved but they think that going to church makes them saved! If you are in doubt whether you are truly saved, I implore you to pause for a second, flip the book to the last page and say the prayer of salvation and stop the devil from stealing from you right now!

(2) **The stony ground:** These are born-again believers who are like spiritual babies. They receive the word with joy but they are

not yet mature and so, they still need time to renew their mind by the word of God so as to grow some roots in themselves.

Therefore, tribulations and persecutions make them fall easily. But, the devil can't steal the word from their hearts directly because they are already saved and so, he tries to use circumstances to rob them. Spiritually, these ones can overcome any thing that comes against them in life but they need time to learn how to walk in the spirit and be led by the Holy Spirit. At this stage, the can rely on more mature believers for guidance, insight, wisdom e t c

All believers must start from this stage but unfortunately, many stop here! Many of the Israelites who left Egypt died in this state of mind. Many Christians stay in this stage, some even die in this stage because they think that becoming born-again is all about going to heaven, but there is far more than just going to heaven. Maturity needs to manifest.

(3) **The ones among thorns:** These are born-again believers who are in the about-to-bear-fruit stage. They have developed from babies into youths. They have renewed some areas of their minds by the word of God. As so, some stony grounds of their hearts have been softened by the word of God. The seed has grown roots, it has matured into a tree but it still needs time to bear fruit. In the main time, the word of God through the Holy Spirit would urge them to remove any other lingering **weeds** in their lives in order to ensure that the word is not choked. These ones have trees but no fruits yet. If they continue in the word by renewing their minds and walking in obedience, they shall surely start bearing fruits.

I personally perceive and believe that quite a considerable

number of Christians are in this category.

(4) **The ones on good ground:** These are born-again believers who are mature. People who manifest the fruits of the Holy Spirit and we see them get the results that the bible talks about. These ones have allowed the word of God to significantly renew their minds and transform their very being. They have allowed the word of God to soften them and remove weeds from their lives. The word has developed roots in them, the roots have dug deep into the soil of their hearts, weeds of sin and un-believe are removed and are daily being removed. **This is where every Christian should at least be!**

The fruit that they bear indicates their level of maturity. I believe that the 30-fold-return indicates the mature fruit-bearing believers who are already getting results but they still have some things to learn and there is always something to learn. The more they yield to the word of God and the Holy Spirit, the more fruit they would bear.

Then, we have the 60-fold-return fruit-bearing mature believers. These have deepened themselves more into the things of God, they have perfected what they have learnt and teach others the same, and they are finally getting ready to step into the roles of spiritual fatherhood and motherhood in the body of Christ.

Then, we have the 100-fold-return fruit-bearing mature believers. These ones have totally yielded their lives to God. They are the spiritual fathers and mothers. These ones have renewed their minds totally that it can be said of them "They have the mind of Christ". In fact, looking at them, one is meant to see Jesus. These ones have left families, husbands, wives, lands, brothers, sisters, houses, strengths, weaknesses, passions, ambitions e t c for the sake of the gospel and surely, they would reap a 100-fold both in this life and in the life to come! Very small percentage of believers is in this category.

Question is: "what category do you belong to?"

Luke 13:7-9

So he said to the man who took care of the vineyard, 'For three years now I've been coming to look for fruit on this fig tree and haven't found any. Cut it down! Why should it use up the soil?' " 'Sir,' the man replied, 'leave it alone for one more year, and I'll dig around it and fertilize it. If it bears fruit next year, fine! If not, then cut it down.' "

If someone has been a believer for three years and have not manifested a single fruit, they need to read that scripture over and over again!

Using our vehicle illustration, the mind is represented by the person who drives the vehicle. If the driver is drunk of wine, then both the vehicle and the passengers are in for a big trouble.

In fact, many road accidents are due to drunk drivers. Nobody would in their right senses board a vehicle if they knew that the driver is drunk yet, many Christians are driving the "temple of God" or "their body" by a "drunken-mindset" or a "carnal mind" which is a mind that disagrees with what God says.

Romans 8:6
For to be carnally minded is death but to be spiritually minded is life and peace.

The bible makes it clear with the scripture above that, a driver who is drunk or carnally-minded will get you killed if you allow him or her to drive you.

Now, because whoever drives the vehicle has total control, the devil being someone that is addicted to being in control, always want to get people off the driver's seat and drive their vehicle or life, if they allow him.

The devil wants to control your mind!

If you hear that someone is demon-possessed, it means that a demon or evil spirit has totally taken over the driver's seat or the mind of that person. Such a person would see themselves doing things that they never thought possible. You ask them 'why did you do it?' and they say, 'I heard a voice that said I should do it!' You hear about them committing suicide, committing murder etc. They are usually demon possessed and they need someone who is anointed by God to forcefully remove the demon or evil spirit off the driver's seat of their vehicle, and have them take control of their vehicle or life again.

If someone says to you "Have you lost your mind?", this is exactly what they mean! You can lose your mind spiritually to an evil spirit. I believe that is one of the reasons why God warned the Israelites never to consult spiritualists or mediums. Those evil spirits are there to rob you of your mind!

At a milder level, some people are demon oppressed, even born-again believers. When someone is being oppressed, what it means is that a demon is sitting at their passenger's seat, making suggestions. It makes strong and persuasive suggestions like: "Hello, sexy guy, why don't you quickly have a look at a sex educating website-pornography. After all, it is good for a man to know how to please his woman ". Or it says to a drug addict, "hello cool guy, you look more confident when you take that thing, don't you? It's really good for your self-esteem. Moreover, just a little bit would not hurt you. "

Every demon-oppressed believer should realize that to get delivered, all they need to do is ask the Lord to help them and more importantly, they need someone who has the power of the Holy Spirit working strong in their live to help them cast that reckless, stinking demon out of their life.

I had a personal experience with this. For a period of about 3 months, I noticed that I had stopped reading my bible and praying due to the high demand of my time and energy from a new job. And so, I noticed that I started watching pornography online. I didn't just start watching it from day one. Recognize! Demons entice you little by little. I started watching lustful online videos to fill the vacuum in my heart because I was not filling myself with the things of God. Then, I graduated to watching movies with high sexual scenes and before I knew it, I was watching pornographic websites every night for about 1 to 3 hours, even 4 hours sometimes. Before this time, I was spending exactly 3 to 4 hours every night in God's presence!

At this time, I knew I needed help because I found it very hard to read my bible even though, in my spirit I wanted to. I would pick up my bible and find it hard to focus. My bible became so boring to read, so tasteless like stale bread. Then one Sunday morning, I decided that enough was enough, and I started praying on the way to church. I started telling the Lord that I was tired of living without studying the bible and enjoying His presence. I said, Lord, please help me because I don't know what is happening. I thought it was a habit problem, I did not even know that I had a demon that was pulling my strings through lustful thoughts!

I got to church and while the pastor was preaching, she started praying in tongues and I noticed that I was now speaking in a very powerful dialect of tongue and then, I fell on my knees, under the power of God, and then while I was lying on the floor and vibrating under the anointing, the pastor started commanding the demon to go, and zoom, it left. One thing that I knew for sure is that the evil spirit had wings because while it was leaving my presence, I was flipping my hands like a chicken that is trying to fly. It was not funny!

Oh my God, the feeling was so good when that demon left. It was opened heavens. I felt like I could pray for many hours and not get tired.

Please recognize this: "the demon was there all the time and I did not know it!" Some Christians have demons oppressing them but they don't even know it! Demons are very deceptive. They make suggestions to you through thoughts and because it sounds like you to you, you think you are the one thinking it, when it is a demon.

Therefore, it is very important that you check every thought in your mind that they agree with the word of God, before you speak or act on them.

2 Corinthians 10: 3-5

"For though we walk in the flesh, we do not war after the flesh:

(For the weapons of our warfare are not carnal, but mighty through God to the pulling down of strong holds;)

Casting down <u>imaginations</u>, and every high thing that exalteth itself against the knowledge of God, and bringing into captivity <u>every thought</u> to the obedience of Christ."

This is a deep revelation. When people are wicked towards you, when people even persecute you, when people steal from you e t c it is not usually the people in a sense but rather, it is the evil spirits in their lives that make the suggestions to them and because usually, they don't even know that those thoughts or suggestions or ideas are from the devil, they act on them. Therefore, you being in the light should not be angry at them, but rather pray for them. Pray for them because they need deliverance from the power of darkness!

By praying for those who persecute you and blessing those who curse you, you don't just get rewarded by God, you actually end up using their evil towards you as an opportunity to advance the kingdom of God. In fact, through your godly obedience, the devil ends up advancing the kingdom of God through you! Think about it!

Luke 6:28

Bless them that curse you, and pray for them which despitefully use you.

When you begin to see life the way the bible says it is, **you are spiritually-minded indeed** and the power of God would be able to flow easily to you and through you.

The word of God-Bible, has the power to clean your mind from every junk of information that you might have come across in life. These days, you can hardly blink your eyes without being bombarded with excessive and idolatry ideas. That is why you need to always clean your mind continuously and also guard yourself every time with the word of God.

Read your bible not just every morning, but every night before going to bed, and every other time you have available. The question should never be when do you read your bible, it should be when do you not read your bible?

Sometimes, when you prove too stubborn to the devil, he would use people close to you, people who would yield to him knowingly or unknowingly, to trigger thoughts in your mind. He would try to use words spoken by friends, enemies, media, education, religion, etc. He seems to have his hand in many places and so, you sole protection is the knowledge of the Word. As soon as you sense a contradiction to the word of God, raise a red-flag! The more you mature as a believer, the easier it would become for you to discern what is good and what is not.

Hebrew 5:14

But solid food is for the mature, who by constant use have trained themselves to distinguish good from evil.

Ephesians 6: 10 - 13

"Finally, be strong in the Lord and in his mighty power. Put on the full armor of God so that you can take your stand against the devil's schemes. For our struggle is not against flesh and blood, but against the rulers, against the authorities, against the

powers of this dark world and against the spiritual forces of evil in the heavenly realms. Therefore put on the full armor of God, so that when the day of evil comes, you may be able to stand your ground, and after you have done everything, to stand."

Therefore, the body is not the problem but it is the kind of mind that drives the body that is the main issue. If the mind is carnal, it would drive the body towards fornication, adultery, covetousness, drunkenness, wild partying, idolatry etc. Whereas, if the mind is spiritual, it would drive the same body towards holiness, self-control, gentleness, love, peace e t c which are called the fruits of the spirit.

Think about it, if you give your vehicle to a thief, he would probably drive it to a place to steal. But if you give it to a drug-addict, he would drive the same vehicle to buy drugs. Yet, if you give the same vehicle to a spirit-filled born-again believer, you will see the same vehicle parked in the Church!

Your body is not the problem; it is the driver or mind that drives your body that is the problem. Renew the mind of a baby believer by studying and doing the word of God day and night and maturity must manifest.

Your Brain
VS
Vehicle Battery

The battery of the vehicle easily compares to the brain of the driver of the vehicle. Both the driver's brain and the vehicle's battery process electric signals. The battery empowers many components of the vehicle before the engine usually takes over. The driver's brain empowers the driver to get things done until his subconscious or spirit takes over. When this happens, he does not even need to consult his brain to change the gears, he just does it automatically.

In essence, as the brain behind the vehicle, you can get things done by using your brain or logic or flesh, but the real power is in your spirit and that is probably why God wants us to live by the spirit and not by the flesh.

Also, a vehicle can initially be empowered from the battery, but the greater power comes from the engine of the vehicle. A vehicle that relies totally on a battery for power would need very big and efficient batteries, and charging those batteries would require so much electricity, and that is why most vehicles rely on the engine rather than the battery for full power. A person that lives on brain knowledge or human intelligence alone needs a very big and efficient brain but unfortunately there is a limit to the size of brain that a man can have. When you run out of wisdom, tap into your spirit in prayer where the wisdom of God is and God would release His wisdom to you!

Therefore, do not live your life only relying on the flesh, it would disappoint you. The people of the world live like this because that is all they know and have, but you know better. Walk in the light as even your heavenly Father is Light, and in Him there is no darkness at all.

Sometimes the battery of a vehicle runs dry and the vehicle refuses to start. In this case, the battery can be changed, or the battery can be recharged or the vehicle has to be jump-started by using jumper-cables.

The jumper-cable allows you to use the power of another vehicle to start your own vehicle. When you start feeling discouraged, tired, and weak so that you can't even pray or believe, you need some jumper-cables my friend! You need someone to help you jump-start your faith. That would get you going for some time, so that you can get yourself refreshed. Because the battery of a vehicle is dead or malfunctioned, does not mean that the engine is faulty.

So also, if the brain of a believer stops them from receiving from God due to many reasons e.g. past experiences, traditions, fatigue, discouragement, circumstances, lack of knowledge e t c, they can get help by being prayed for by friends and other believers.

An example is found in the gospel which goes thus:

Mark 9:20-26

"So they brought him. When the spirit saw Jesus, it immediately threw the boy into a convulsion. He fell to the ground and rolled around, foaming at the mouth. Jesus asked the boy's father, "How long has he been like this?" "From childhood," he answered. "It has often thrown him into fire or water to kill him. But if you can do anything, take pity on us and help us." " 'If you can'?" said Jesus. "Everything is possible for him who believes."

Immediately the boy's father exclaimed, "I do believe; help me overcome my unbelief!" When Jesus saw that a crowd was running to the scene, he rebuked the evil spirit. "You deaf and mute spirit," he said, "I command you, come out of him and never enter him again." The spirit shrieked, convulsed him violently and came out. The boy looked so much like a corpse that many said, "He's dead."

The man believed from his heart or spirit or engine, that Jesus Christ could heal the boy. In fact, his mind agreed with the fact that Jesus Christ could heal the boy, but something was in him that made him have some unbelief, and I believe this was his brain, logic, tradition, religion, experience e t c I believe that the man's logic kept telling him "Your son has been deaf and dumb since childhood ! It is rather too late for him to get healed now." Therefore, Jesus had to by-pass his brain by attaching some jumper cables on him spiritually, and just like that, the power was released! When we hold hands and pray with other believers who are weaker than us, believing with them for an answer to a prayer, we are helping them jump-start their faith.

Talking about jumper-cables, this takes us to an interesting point. As a believer, you need people around you who can pray with you and for you. People that you share your victories and challenges with.

SMALL QUIZ

What do you think represents such people in your vehicle?

Your Faith Friends VS Vehicle Four Wheels

Mark 2: 3-5

"Some men came, bringing to him a paralytic, carried by <u>four</u> of them. Since they could not get him to Jesus because of the crowd, they made an opening in the roof above Jesus and, after digging through it, lowered the mat the paralyzed man was lying on. When Jesus saw their faith, he said to the paralytic, "Son, your sins are forgiven.""

Jesus also had a very close relationship to 4 disciples namely: Simon Peter, Andrew, James and John.

The top scripture reveals some truths. Four men carried a friend who was paralytic-could not walk. Using the analogy of the vehicle, the body of the vehicle is usually carried by 4 wheels. The vehicle itself is stationary unless it is carried by the wheels. Brothers and Sisters, we need people devoted to praying for us, even as we pray for them!

The four wheels of the vehicle must agree. They must flow in agreement with the power that is released from the engine.

They must be free from wear and tear. In fact, one of the greatest vehicle accidents happen when one wheel or more, busts while a vehicle is at a top speed on the highway.

Brothers and Sisters, we need friends who share our belief. People who can pray with us and for us. Friends who themselves are willing to move forward. Imagine if two wheels of a vehicle decide to move forward, and the other two decide to move backwards, there would be stagnation, overheating, waste of energy, and I would not be surprised if the engine gets knocked.

While I pressed full stop to pause for a moment, I thought to myself, what else can I write, and just in time, some scriptures came to my mind.

Proverbs 6:19b
The Lord hates one who sows discord among brethren.

Proverbs 27:17
As iron sharpens iron, so a man sharpens the countenance of his friend.

God wants believers to be together, to pray together, to celebrate together, to share together, to mourn together, because when we are together, God is there and because God wants to be with us, He wants us to be together. The coming together of believers is called the Church. When people are one in God, **there is nothing or no one that can stop them.**

Deuteronomy 32:30
How could one chase a thousand, and two put ten thousand to flight, unless their Rock had sold them, and the Lord had surrendered them?

Nimrod in the book of genesis, chapter 11, is a man that led very many people together in oneness, to build a tower. The bible accounts that the people were one and nothing that they purposed to do was impossible. Yes, nothing was impossible for them, but it was deniable. God being the Ultimate Ruler, knew that what they tried to do was possible for them, but He denied them by confusing them. Oh Lord, My God, my soul cries out to the day when the whole body of Christ would pray together as one, and on that day, the kingdom of darkness would fall like a pack of cards!

The word of God says, when two or more are gathered together in my name, there I am. Now, when a man and woman gather together and become husband and wife, in the name of Jesus, we call them family. That means, in every family that is joined together in the name of Jesus, He is always there in their midst.

When a family of say a husband and wife with or without their children live together, Jesus is there. Imagine a nation where from house to house, you see families in their households who are joined together in the name of Jesus! Surely such a nation is blessed because blessed is the nation whose God is the Lord!

Dear Reader, have a list of believing friends but select a strong-four team who you can share your expectations, disappointments, struggles and victories with.

Psalm 133:1
Behold, how good and how pleasant it is for brethren to dwell together in unity.

Be totally free and transparent with these carefully selected believing friends even as they are open to you. Jesus Christ prayed over-night before selecting his disciples. Pray about whom your strong-four should be and share with them, support them, pray for them, celebrate with them.

Finally, if the governments of nations make it compulsory that every vehicle must have an extra wheel in case of unpredictable failures, then, you can as well be on the look-out for at least a potential believer, should one of your strong-four have to leave for reasons beyond control.

This happened in the book of Acts after Judas Iscariot betrayed Jesus. Apostle Peter and the other 10 disciples prayed to God for whom they should choose to replace Judas, and Matthias was chosen!

When we talk about praying, it would be incomplete without talking about the Holy Spirit. The next chapter sheds some light on the Holy Spirit.

SMALL QUIZ

We said earlier that the spark-plug of a vehicle symbolizes the "fire" function of the Holy Spirit. What symbolizes the "leading" function of the Holy Spirit in a vehicle?

Your Helper – Holy Spirit VS Vehicle Navigation System

Romans 8:14

As many as are led by the Holy Spirit, they shall be called the sons of God.

We mentioned earlier that the spark-plug in the engine of a vehicle represents one of the functions of the Holy Spirit. Did you notice that before you became a born again, reading your bible felt dry and lifeless?

2 Corinthians 3:16

He has made us competent as ministers of a new covenant— not of the letter but of the Spirit; for the letter kills, but the Spirit gives life.

How did "the word of God" even become the "living word"? The power of the Holy Spirit overshadowed the "receiver of the word of God"- Mary, and she conceived the living word- Jesus.

The Holy Spirit burns the word of God in your spirit and releases the power in the word. When God said in the beginning, "Let there be light", that statement carried the power of fulfillment in itself, but it takes the Holy Spirit to unleash that power.

God created all things by His spoken word, and the spoken word is executed by the Holy Spirit. If the Holy Spirit therefore created all things - both visible and invisible, then no man can ever explain the mystery of the Holy Spirit and this chapter would only try as much as the Holy Spirit Himself inspires, because the Holy Spirit is the greatest teacher.

John 14:26
But the Helper, the Holy Spirit, whom the Father will send in My name, He will teach you all things, and bring to your remembrance all things that I said to you.

And so, the spark-plug in the engine represents one of the countless functions of the Holy Spirit. As God said:" I am that I am", it follows that, the Holy Spirit can be who He wants to be and He can also function like the navigation system of a vehicle. In fact, I am fully persuaded that the idea of a navigation system in the technological industry is inspired by the Holy Spirit Himself.

In the time past, people drove by mapping the roads in their mind. These days, with new technologies, all you need is a navigation system, and you are ready to roll. Browsing online, you can get a good navigator for just £70. Good luck to you if your vehicle already has one installed.

Like Barnabas in the book of Acts, it was as if he got one installed immediately. After becoming born-again, he and his family got baptized in the Holy Spirit and started speaking in tongues. One of the numerous roles of the Holy Spirit in the life of a believer is to give us direction in our lives. It is amazing how the navigation system works. When you miss the way, it says: 'Turn around, turn to the left, after 200 yards, turn to the right'.

Isaiah 30:21

Whether you turn to the right or to the left, your ears will hear a voice behind you, saying, "This is the way; walk in it."

Also, just like the navigation searches for the shortest route to a destination, so does the Holy Spirit searches the heart of God to reveal the will of God to us. The same way a navigation system requires you to enter your destination, the Holy Spirit requires us to enter our destination as "**The Will of God Avenue**".

1 Corinthians 2: 5-10

'However, as it is written:
"No eye has seen, no ear has heard, no mind has conceived what God has prepared for those who love him", but God has revealed it to us by his Spirit. The Spirit <u>searches</u> all things, even the deep things of God.'

Also, the navigation system allows you to know where you are located physically on the earth, whether you are in oxford street, London or in London Road, Oxford. While the Holy Spirit lets you know where you are on the scale of holiness, forgiveness, self-control, love e t c.

The navigation system shows you roads to come. The Holy Spirit reveals the future to you.

The navigation system directs your paths to your destination while the Holy Spirit leads you to your destiny or calling or purpose in life.

It is not everybody that becomes a born-again that immediately gets baptized in the Holy-spirit and start speaking in tongues but believe me, it is a very important stage in every believer's life. There is also a water baptism which is different from the Holy Spirit baptism. I personally got baptized with the Holy Spirit before I did my water baptism. I noticed that after I did my water baptism though, the Holy Spirit started flowing through me more powerfully than before I did my water baptism. Jesus gave his approval on water baptism and so, it is important to do it.

Luke 11:13
If you then, though you are evil, know how to give good gifts to your children, how much more will your Father in heaven give the Holy Spirit to those who ask Him!

Notice what The Word of God says. How much more will He give us the **Holy Spirit**! Not, how much more will He give us a house or husband or job or ministry or health or joy or wife or e t c

Stop asking for things but start asking God to fill you with the Holy Spirit because when you have the Holy Spirit, they car, house, wife, husband, children, health e t c must show up!

The parable of a traveler that sees a land with a precious hidden jewel comes to mind. He sold everything to buy that land. Brothers and sisters, resist all hindrances and ask for the Holy Spirit, receive the Holy Spirit, fellowship with the Holy Spirit and then, you will have the direction to all things that pertain to life, more than you can ever thing or imagine.

Earthly fathers give gifts to their children but our Heavenly

Father gives us the "giver of all gifts" - the Holy Spirit! Have you heard of the gifts of the Holy Spirit? They are gifts that the Holy Spirit delivers to the children of God, from God through Jesus Christ.

The Holy Spirit has an inexhaustible storehouse of gifts and He is more than willing to give them to us after all, gifts are meant to be given. This reminds me of a popular movie called Aladdin. Aladdin was a being that provided all the wishes of his master. We are not the master of the Holy Spirit, He created us, but He is delighted to gift us.

Just a quick talk on the gifts of the Holy Spirit.

When someone gives you a gift, your part is simply to receive it and use it. When you get baptized in the Holy Spirit, it is evident by speaking in tongues. Speaking in tongues is simply one of the numerous gifts of the Holy Spirit but you have to receive it by faith and use it by faith. You receive the gifts of the Holy Spirit by faith, and therefore, your role is to do the using. You have to do the speaking when gifted with speaking in tongues because the Holy Spirit will not do the speaking for you!

If someone gave you money and they do the spending for you, what is the point in giving it to you anyways! You have to do the spending!

The Holy Spirit chooses to gift some people when He created them in their mother's womb. We call them the naturally gifted. Yet, even the most naturally gifted would not prosper in their gifting unless they use it.

I know the day when the Holy Spirit imparted me with the gift of writing. It was in September of 2009, at Notting Hill Gate, London, at the Kensington Temple Church's 7pm Revival Service. The Holy Spirit ministered to me that night, and while in the bus going home, all I wanted to do was just write and write and write. I could not stop, I had to write something. I had the feeling, because the Holy Spirit gave me the gift, but I had to do the writing.

Have you got a gift? If yes, then start using it.

Apostle Peter and John, when they heard that some gentiles had become believers in the book of Acts, they travelled down to meet them from Jerusalem, just to make sure that these ones receive the Holy Spirit by the laying of hands. Apostle Peter and John knew how important it was to have the Holy Spirit in the life of a believer, and so they endeavored to travel down to lay hands on them.

Yet, in this day and age, we have religious groups teaching that the Holy Spirit left with the last apostles. Yet, the Holy spirit inspired this very book because the writer himself is a nobody, who simply was found by Jesus, and as Jesus said to Peter," Prepare a small boat for me, that I might preach from it to the People ". All that the Lord wants is someone who is willing to be small, so that the Lord might prove Himself Big to them and through them. When Jesus Christ said "Tarry in Jerusalem, that you may be endured with Power from on High", He meant what he said. The Lord is looking for men and women, who would separate themselves to Him, who are willing to be a small boat so that He can minister to them and through them. Men and women who would tarry in Jerusalem- in the place of prayer and worship, in the presence of God and in the word of God, so that they can be clothed with Power from on high, so that the world might see Jesus Christ in them and through them, not just in words but in deeds!

Apostle Paul said "May the love of God, the grace of our Lord Jesus Christ and the fellowship of the Holy Spirit be with you, now and forever more".

The fellowship of the Holy Spirit is so important. The Holy Spirit is the presence of God and when you learn to dwell in that presence, you are protected, you are empowered, you are refreshed, you are transformed and you learn to hear the voice of God etc. And guess what? The devil does not like you to go into that presence because that is the place where you are empowered to beat the devil.

Let us take a quick visit to psalm 91 for a brief understanding of fellowship of the Holy Spirit.

(**First Verse**) - He who dwells in the secret place of the Most High, ...
(**Last Verse**) - With long life will I satisfy him and show him My salvation.

God is saying dwell in my presence first and finally your salvation (eternal life, prosperity, health, victory, dominion, joy e t c) must show up! Stop seeking your health, spouse, wealth, joy, fulfilled life, success e t c from the world "the tree of knowledge of good and evil" but rather seek for all of these in His presence "the tree of life"!

For He Himself said to you in Matthew 6:33
Seek Yee first the kingdom of God and His righteousness and all these things shall be added to you.

Millions are led by navigation systems every day. Why? Because they make it easy to drive to places that you don't have directions to. Do you want to drive to a place of prosperity, joyful marriage, good health, peace e t c but you just don't know the direction to them? Just allow the Holy Spirit to lead you there.

Behold, brothers and sisters, Jesus is the way – the way to a joyful marriage, the way to prosperity, the way to divine health and healing, the way to everything good in life. The Holy Spirit is the one that would lead you to the way that you must go. Think about it, who led you to Jesus – the way? It was the Holy Spirit! He has been leading you already, but He wants to do it more. God is looking forward to those who would allow the Holy Spirit to lead them in every single area of their lives.

Romans 8:14
As many as are led by the Holy Spirit, they shall be called the sons of God.

And the Holy Spirit led Jesus into the wilderness and He came with Power. Brothers and sisters, be sensitive and obey the promptings of the Holy Spirit. The world is waiting for you to minister to them in power and authority. The Holy Spirit is so important in the life of a believer that Jesus Himself said to the disciples not to go preaching until they have received the power of the Holy Spirit. I pray that may we become people who demonstrate the power of the Holy Spirit and not just people who talk about His power. May we become people who testify that Jesus lives by the demonstration of His power in our finances, ministry, health, children e t c. The world is tired of hearing our blessed confessions without any physical evidences.

1 Corinthians 2:4

And my speech and my preaching were not with persuasive words of human wisdom, but in demonstration of the Spirit and of power...

We have talked about a number of things about vehicles, but hold on a minute, vehicles need fuel to function! Let's talk about the fuel now.

Your Bible Study
VS
Vehicle Fuel

Daniel 1:8
But Daniel purposed in his heart that he would not defile himself with the portion of the king's delicacies, nor with the wine which he drank; therefore he requested of the chief of the eunuchs that he might not defile himself.

In the scripture above, Daniel refused to feed himself with the same kind of information, entertainment, news, movies, magazines e t c that the king of the world system- the devil with his wicked children feed themselves on. Daniel knew that the diet would defile him. Rather, he chose the diet that God says is good. Daniel was spiritually-minded!

Many Christians are aware when the fuel tank of their vehicle is flashing for a refill, but they are usually not aware when their spiritual tank is empty.

A simple indication to me that my spiritual tank is getting empty is when I start acting unfriendly, depressed, craving lustfully in my mind, acting in envy, being unforgiving, easily offended e t c

If at these moments I do not bombard my mind with high dosages of the word of God, I would start getting hooked to sinful materials and start resenting reading the bible, or going to church and before I know it, I am already the prodigal son! Although, I have learnt to never hesitate to go back home to my heavenly Father in prayer, no matter how badly I could have slipped.

I have also recognized that because God loved me before I became born-again by giving me His only begotten Son, how much more when I have given my life to Christ! I might have struggles but God knew who I was before He saved me. When I presented myself to Him to get saved, He did not look at me like a vehicle repairer and say
"This one is beyond repairs, it has to be scrapped!" No! He said: "I love you, you are the apple of my eye, enter into the pleasure of your Lord". Therefore, I always go into the presence of God and tell Him about my struggles and victories and He always strengthens me.

Hebrews 4: 15 - 16
"For we do not have a High Priest who cannot sympathize with our weaknesses, but was in all points tempted as we are, yet without sin. Let us therefore come boldly to the throne of grace, that we may obtain mercy and find grace to help in time of need".

Please let us analyze this scripture just a little bit.

<u>...but was in all points tempted as we are, yet without sin.</u>
Brothers and sisters, Jesus was tempted not just in many points but in all points as we are today, therefore He understands the temptations that you go through and He knows How to

overcome them because He was without sin. Never ever try to fight your temptations by yourself alone.

Let us therefore come boldly to the throne of grace.

He said boldly because He knows that there are chances that we would feel condemned or guilty or ashamed e t c but He said come boldly!

...that we may obtain mercy and find grace.

Mercy awaits you every time you fail in your walk with God, and there is grace at the throne of God as well. Grace is like a gift, an empowerment that can allow you to walk over your temptations and challenges etc.

...to help in time of need.

Brothers and sisters, there are **times of need** in our walk with Jesus, but Jesus is saying "be of good cheer, I have overcome the world."

Don't try to be a super-Christian who is so powerful that he can get rid of his sinful nature by himself. The arm of flesh would fail you. If you could not save yourself from the kingdom of darkness by your own works or righteousness, what makes you think you can get rid of your sinful nature by your own power? It is by grace through faith that you were saved, not by works. Your sinful nature would be conquered by grace and not by works!

People are aware that normally you have to fill up the vehicle with fuel. Depending on how far a journey is going to be, the more fuel you have to put in. Cities have gas stations where you can easily fill up vehicles with fuel. These days, online maps even show you where the closest gas station is to you.

Luke 5:15
So He Himself often withdrew into the wilderness and prayed.

Filling up your tank is simply studying the word of God- your bible, listening to biblical preaching and teachings. It is simply making spiritual energy available. It is like eating food to the body. Physical food provides physical energy; the word of God provides spiritual energy. Do you know that when you are really physically hungry, you can hardly do anything, but when you fill yourself up, you want to leap rather than walk? When you are spiritually hungry, you can neither pray nor praise God, but when you fill up yourself, you are not just praying and praising God, you are actually dancing in His presence!

Ecclesiastes 8:4
Where the word of a king is, there is power.

John 6:63b
The words that I speak to you are spirit, and they are life.

Proverbs 18:21a
Death and life are in the power of the tongue...

Psalms 107:20
He sent His word and healed them and delivered them from their destructions.

Many of us know how much it costs us to fuel a vehicle. Most of us know that filling a vehicle with just 5 liters will hardly last us for more than a day, yet we devote just 5 minutes a day to the bible and we expect it to take us through the day. We spend more time taking breakfast than reading the bible. Most people would spend around 15minutes on breakfast, then a drink here and some pieces of fruits there, until lunch time when a big meal of takeaway is the norm. Then, in the evening, we grab a bottle of drink and 3 pieces of snack, till we get home for a properly cooked dinner, ending it with perhaps some deserts.

Now, consider someone who wakes up in the morning, eats a bowl of cereal with no milk, and eats nothing all day long, gets home, sleep, and continues like that for weeks or perhaps months or years. That would be suicidal you would agree and yet, many Christians live like this. Perhaps, they get a big meal of readymade spiritual food from their Church every Sunday, hoping that the Sunday-takeaway is enough to last them for the whole week!

Yet, they would never live like that in the physical. They know that such a lifestyle would make them vulnerable to sickness and diseases. They know that it would weaken them and they know that it would stop them from enjoying life. Are we surprised why the church is presently full of many unfruitful believers? If a child is malnourished, simply change his or her diet.

Some people see malnourished children on the television and think, whoa, they need some food. Yet, they themselves look exactly like that, or even worse in the spirit. We need spiritual mirrors to see ourselves, and the bible is that mirror.

James 1: 23 - 24

Anyone who listens to the word but does not do what it says is like a man who looks at his face in a <u>mirror</u> and, after looking at himself, goes away and immediately forgets what he looks like.

But my dear reader, I am confident that you are not like that because you study your bible every day because you know that like a vehicle, if it has no fuel, it has no power, if it has no power, it becomes stagnant, if it becomes stagnant for too long and the rain begins to fall on it, it gives way to rust and from there, it ends up in the scrape yard.

John 15:2
"Every branch in me that does not bear fruit he takes away, and every branch that does bear fruit he prunes, that it may bear more fruit."

Luke 14: 34-35
"Salt is good; but if the salt has lost its flavor, how shall it be seasoned? It is neither fit for the land nor for the dunghill, but men throw it out. He who has ears to hear, let him hear!"

Feeding yourself daily is very basic yet people struggle with it. The devil does not mind that you go to church as long as you never have time to study your bible yourself. He knows that like the vehicle, your spiritual walk with God will be stagnant if you rely only on ready-made teachings from pastors and preachers.

Sure, reading other people's revelations is good, if it were not good, nobody would be inspired by the Holy Spirit to write Christian books and even the bible was inspired by the Holy Spirit.

Also, many are the ministers who have through their ministries helped even me to improve my understanding of the things of God. Nevertheless, my greatest lessons were learnt by fellowshipping with the Holy Spirit directly, and that is where this book in particular was given birth to. So, you need to sit at the foot of Jesus, and have a personal and continuous relationship with Jesus through the Holy Spirit.

That reminds me of a short story in the bible that goes thus:

Luke 10:38-42
As Jesus and his disciples were on their way, he came to a village where a woman named Martha opened her home to him. She had a sister called Mary, who sat at the Lord's feet listening to what he said. But Martha was distracted by all the preparations that had to be made. She came to him and asked, "Lord, don't you care that my sister has left me to do the work by myself? Tell her to help me!"
"Martha, Martha," the Lord answered, "you are worried and upset about many things, but only one thing is needed. Mary has chosen what is better, and it will not be taken away from her."

So, please devote at least 30 minutes early in the morning after waking up, and at least 30 minutes in the night before sleeping to study your bible and see yourself grow.

It sounds very simple but expect the devil to try all schemes and deceptions, distractions e t c, behold all hell break loose because he knows that ones you have the word in you, the world can be taken by you. A simple tip is to switch off your phones, postpone all seemingly urgent matters and learn to spend time with God alone. If you can do this consistently, you can do all things through Christ Jesus who strengthens you.

This brings up an interesting topic. If you live in a western society, you would be aware that these days, you can drive into a fuel or gas station, fill up the tank of your vehicle, and then walk into the office to pay, or perhaps pay at the machine using a credit or debit card. Because people could take advantage of this system, monitoring cameras are installed in almost all gas stations, which record every single event. Then, you will notice the sign that says the following:

It is a criminal offence to fill up the tank of your vehicle without paying.

You will be prosecuted if you do this.

It is good to read the bible on your own, but it is even better if you have a local church where you are planted and rooted, where you are trained and impacted, where you are edified because for these reasons Jesus Christ gave some to be apostles, some evangelists, some prophets, some pastors and some teachers for the edification of the whole body, which is the church.

Just like a child has a family where he or she is taken care of, you as a spiritual child need a spiritual family of God where you can be nurtured.

Therefore when you learn from a minister of God who ministers biblically, and you know that you are being truly fed, you own it a responsibility to pay for that spiritual meal that they offer you.

You must pay your tithe to the church that feeds you.

When you fill up your vehicle at the station without paying, you are unfair to the workers at that station, you are unfair to the driver of the truck who drives long miles to bring that fuel down to the station, you are unfair to the company that processes that fuel into diesel or petrol, you are unfair to the workers at the oil rigs who dig up the petroleum from the ground, you are unfair to the company that invested billions to put it all together, you are unfair to the government because you deny them the tax that is already included in that fuel price and finally you are unfair to yourself because you will surely be caught !

Now, if the world system can be so orderly as to ensure that nobody takes advantage easily, how do you think the kingdom of God would be?

Some Christians have received their spiritual letters of prosecution. They have even received their verdict but yet, they are not aware of this because they are spiritually blind. Have they not read the book of Malachi?

(Malachi 3: 8 - 12)
"Will a man rob God? Yet you rob me. "But you ask, 'How do we rob you?' "In tithes and offerings. You are under a curse—the whole nation of you—because you are robbing me.

Bring the whole tithe into the storehouse, that there may be food in my house. Test me in this," says the LORD Almighty, "and see if I will not throw open the floodgates of heaven and pour out so much blessing that you will not have room enough for it. I will prevent pests from devouring your crops, and the vines in your fields will not cast their fruit," says the LORD Almighty.

"Then all the nations will call you blessed, for yours will be a delightful land," says the LORD Almighty.

If we always pay for our food takeaways, then, we should never forget to pay for our spiritual food takeaways as well because, it takes time and effort to prepare this food for you. Years of learning, experimenting, trying, failing, winning, growing, fasting, praying, laboring, forgiving, reading e t c all of these is packaged for you by your minister in a 30 minute or 1 hour easy-to-understand service!

Just try yourself to prepare a 10-minute message from the bible in a way that would minister to the needs of the congregation and see how easy it is! It is the Holy Spirit that does the teaching but if the minister does not make himself or herself available, who would the Holy Spirit minister through?

When you pay your tithes and offerings, you make it possible for God to bless you especially in your finances and the church needs you blessed so that you can finance the gospel. What did Jesus Christ even say about tithes ?

Luke 11:42
But woe to you Pharisees! For you tithe mint and rue and all manner of herbs and pass by justice and the love of God. These you ought to have done, **without leaving the others undone**.

I believe that the statement Jesus made above in the gospel of Luke simply settles it!

Finally, the bible says that without faith, it is impossible to please God. Therefore, even if you pay your tithes and offerings, if you don't do it by faith, it would not be pleasing to God and you might not get a harvest, and since we want you to always get a bountiful harvest from God, we shall be talking about faith in the next chapter.

Your Faith
VS
Vehicle Gears

Hebrews 11:6

And **without faith** it **is** impossible to please God, because anyone who comes to Him must believe that He exists and that He rewards those who earnestly seek Him.

Until we engage the gears of faith in the vehicle of our destiny, we move not.

I heard someone once say: "Have you ever seen Christians who do not walk by faith, yet they have the Holy Spirit in them? He said that they are like when someone starts a vehicle engine, they leave the gear of the vehicle at neutral and press the accelerator. You hear how powerful the vehicle is, you hear the loud power gushing out from that vehicle, you imagine how fast that vehicle would move if it were released and then you realize all of a sudden that the vehicle with all that power has not moved just one bit. You hear such believers speak in tongues and fall under the anointing and when you look into their personal lives, you see no manifestations of the power of God. Instead of divine health, you see sickness, instead of provision, you see lack, instead of victors you see victims, instead of dominion you see captivity, and you wonder why this so? "

After hearing this, the Holy Spirit gave me a revelation.

As there are different levels of gears in a vehicle, so also, are there different levels of faith. When you start a vehicle, you need to start from gear one upwards. Gear one allows the vehicle to move from "no-motion" or stationary to motion. Once the vehicle is moving, more power is available and the vehicle can now go on to gear 2, which is a faster and more powerful level. At this stage, the navigation system would give instructions and the driver would apply the brake or accelerate or turn the steering or depending on the situations, the driver could decide to engage higher levels of the gears.

So also, in our walk of faith as believers, we must first operate at the very first level of faith before we can qualify to operate at the higher levels of faith. If you are not faithful in little things, who will entrust you with the big things? If you cannot be faithful in cleaning the church, who will entrust you with the power to clean up the "temple of God" by casting out demons ! David was faithful in keeping a few flocks of sheep and God chose him to lead the nation of Israel.

Some gears hardly ever gets used in some countries like the UK, where they have speed limits and speed cameras almost everywhere, but where I come from which is Nigeria, every gear is up for use! Hallelujah! Can this be the reason why when a Nigerian is on fire for God, **HE OR SHE IS REALLY ON FIRE**? We Nigerians use all the gears available without any restraints whatsoever!

In essence, your environment can affect the level of faith that you operate in. In fact, Jesus Christ, when he wanted to heal a blind man in Bethsaida, because of the lack of faith in that town was so high, Jesus had to hold that blind man by the hand, and take him out of the town before he healed him.

Even after praying for him, the guy was so full of unbelief that he saw men as trees, and then Jesus prayed for him again and he received his healing.

Mark 8:26
"Then He sent him away to his house, saying, "Neither go into the town, nor tell anyone in the town.""

Jesus is saying to many in the body of Christ that:
"the level of faith that I need you to walk in requires that you change your environment, because your environment changes your way of thinking, and as a man thinks, so is he".

Jesus is saying to some people:
"You need to change your friends, your job, your residence, your lifestyle, your level of devotion, your denomination, your traditions, your beliefs e t c in order to operate in the faith or anointing that I have for you ".

May God give us an obedient and willing heart, (Amen).

Someone could ask, so what is symbolic of gear one in faith walking? I asked the Holy Spirit the same question and I believe He said to me that your finance is the least - the first gear that allows you to practice your faith. If the birds of the sky and beasts of the land can trust God for provision, then you must be able to trust God to provide for you! If the unclean ravens could tithe and offer the meat and bread to Prophet Elijah and those ravens believe that God would open the windows of Heaven for them, then what about you the child of the Most High? You must be willing to trust God even though your finances might seem insufficient, that by paying your tithe, God would use your seemingly insufficient five loaves of bread to feed five thousand and still allow you have 12 baskets left.

This reminds me of the parable in Luke 18:18-30.

A certain ruler asked Him, "Good teacher, what must I do to inherit eternal life?" "Why do you call me good?" Jesus answered. "No one is good—except God alone. You know the commandments: 'Do not commit adultery, do not murder, do not steal, do not give false testimony, honor your father and mother.'"

"All these I have kept since I was a boy," he said.

When Jesus heard this, he said to him, "You still lack one thing. Sell everything you have and give to the poor, and you will have treasure in heaven. Then come, follow me."

When he heard this, he became very sad, because he was a man of great wealth. Jesus looked at him and said, "How hard it is for the rich to enter the kingdom of God!

Indeed, it is easier for a camel to go through the eye of a needle than for a rich man to enter the kingdom of God."

Those who heard this asked, "Who then can be saved?" Jesus replied, "What is impossible with men is possible with God."

Peter said to him, "We have left all we had to follow you!" "I tell you the truth," Jesus said to them, "no one who has left home or wife or brothers or parents or children for the sake of the kingdom of God will fail to receive many times as much in this age and, in the age to come, eternal life."

The ruler does not trust the Lord enough to rely on the Lord for provision and yet, he wants to rely on the Lord for salvation.

Which is greater, provision or salvation? Salvation contains provision, protection, healing, life etc. Jesus said in the scriptures below:

Matthew 23:17
"Fools and blind! For which is greater, the gold or the temple that sanctifies the gold?"

Luke 16:11
"Therefore if you have not been faithful in the unrighteous mammon, who will commit to your trust the true riches?"

Many in the Church today claim they trust the Lord for their salvation but they do not trust him for their provision. They do not tithe to the Lord, they do not support the work of the Lord and they wonder why their spiritual, emotional, financial lives e t c seem stagnant.

Also, the first temptation that the devil threw at Jesus was based on provision. He was simply saying, don't wait upon the Lord when you have power to help yourself, why should you seek God's will when you have your own will and need, why look up to God when you can look to your own strength, why trust God when you can trust yourself, why believe in God for provision when you can provide for yourself, why worship God when you can worship yourself.

Dear reader, I am sure that you are not like this because you love the Lord, you support the ministry of the Lord, you pay your tithe and offering to the house of the Lord, and the Lord blesses you and anoints you because you are found to be faithful.

Someone might ask: ' I already operate at gear one, I already pay my tithe and offering, I even serve the Lord in a ministry and so, what is gear two? I felt the Holy Spirit say:

"Let them ask me themselves!"

Finally, faith is simply trusting in God. The Lord is presently inspiring me to write a book on faith, but just to keep it simple, kindly permit me to touch it on the surface.

Every time you make an order online for example, buying a television, you pay for it online and they promise to deliver that television within a period of time.

Now, before the tv arrives, you begin to imagine where the tv would be placed, you make sure that there would be someone at home to receive the tv delivery. You are already telling your friends about your new tv because you saw and read what that tv is all about, and for sure, the tv is delivered to you.

Now, the company promised you that they would deliver the tv to you. You don't know whether they have the tv in stock, except for the fact that they promised again that it is in stock.

And then, they asked you to pay them for promising you, and you without a shadow of doubt, believed them, paid them and even said thank you for a promise that is yet to be fulfilled.

Then, you did not just believe them, you re-arranged your living room to accommodate the coming new tv. I can see your friends entering your living room and asking you why the re-arrangement of the room and you say to them: "I am hoping the company would fulfill their promise to deliver the tv that I ordered online". NO! NO!! NO!!! You say to your friends "so and so dot com is delivering my new tv on Friday, and I would be placing it over there!"

Friends, that is called faith in the promises of man. If man, who can lie promised and we believe without doubting, what about God?

We need to get to the level where whatever we see in the bible that God promised us, we simply believe it and receive it.

But you say to me, it is different because you saw the tv online, you saw the picture, you even read about its product details, you saw reviews of people who had bought it before, so you knew what you were buying e t c

Sure, you read the reviews of the people who have bought the tv before you buy it. So also, the review of what you want to receive from God is really the testimonies of the people who have received such miracles from God as well.

And right, you saw the tv before you decided to buy it. When God promises you something, you also have to see it spiritually before you can receive it. You have to see it through the eyes of faith or through your spiritual eyes. Therefore, we shall talk about "spiritual eyes" in the next chapter.

SMALL QUIZ
What symbolizes "your spiritual eyes" in a vehicle?

Your Spiritual Eyes
VS
Vehicle Lights

Ephesians 1:17 - 18

"I keep asking that the God of our Lord Jesus Christ, the glorious Father, may give you the Spirit of wisdom and revelation, so that you may know him better. I pray also that the eyes of your heart may be enlightened in order that you may know the hope to which he has called you, the riches of his glorious inheritance in the saints,"

We indicated earlier that your heart here does not mean your blood-pumping-organ but rather your spiritual heart, because man is a spirit, he has a soul and he lives in a body.

In the spirit, you have eyes in the spirit to see spiritual things, just like you have eyes in your body to see physical things. In fact, living by faith in God is simply living by what you see spiritually rather than just what you see physically.

When God says to you, "By His stripes, You were healed", God is not talking about your body because your body is not you, you are a spirit, and as far as God is concerned, you are healed because your spirit is healed. It is now left for you to convert that spiritual reality into a physical reality.

So, what do you use to convert a spiritual thing into a physical thing? Your words! When you truly believe what God says about you, when faith is released in your spirit, when you see it in your spirit, just like the online television which you saw so clearly, your healing would look so clear and substantial that you will begin to confess that "I am healed".

Now the bible makes it clear that "The power of life and death is in the tongue", and also Jesus Christ said "By your words, you will be justified or condemned". In fact the book of Hebrews calls Jesus "the high priest of our confession". When you say it because you believe it from your heart, believe me reader, it will come to past in the physical.

Your words are dimension converters that turn the spiritual into the physical.

In fact, there is a negative aspect of this where evil people convert negative <u>spiritual</u> things into the <u>physical</u> by casting spells or curses! This is practiced by witches and voodoo doctors e t c

Why do you think Adam and Eve fell? After eating that forbidden fruit, evil thoughts were activated in their mind, and because a man's thoughts determine his words and his words determine his life. They were calling those things that were not yet there physically, as if they were, and those things had to manifest because the power in their tongue converts the spiritual into the physical.

God said, **"Let there be light, and there was light"**. When God spoke, He spoke spiritually because God is a spirit, and the light manifested in the physical.

God gave us the same ability when He breathed into the nostrils of man and man became a living being!

In fact, let us quickly visit Genesis 2:23.

Adam saw his wife and said:
"This is now bone of my bones and flesh of my flesh.
She shall be called Woman because she was taken out of Man."

After this time, they ate the fruit and when God called Adam, he said in Genesis 3:10

"I heard your voice in the garden and I was <u>afraid</u> because I was <u>naked</u>; and I <u>hid</u> myself."

If you compare the two statements, you would notice that the first statement was a revelation but the second statement indicates negatives. In fact, in the second statement alone, I observed 3 negative words!

Never confess negative words my friends, you are better off keeping quiet. Better still, confess what God says about you.

Back to the spiritual eyes in the vehicle. The front lights flash into the front or future to reveal hidden situations that are about to happen, while the rear lights flash into the back or past to clarify situations that happened in the past.

The lights of the vehicle are always there, but they need to be switched on before they are activated. So also do our spiritual eyes need to be switched on, so that through the Holy Spirit, God can show us secrets. And that was one of the prayers that Apostle Paul was mentioning in Ephesians 1:17 - 18.

The front lights of a vehicle shine into the darkness to reveal all the dangers that are ahead before the vehicle gets there. So also, our spiritual eyes see things that are yet to happen in our journey of life. In my own personal experience, when I am seeking God with all my heart through prayers, devotions, worship and sometimes fasting, my spiritual eyes are activated or switched on and God would start showing me things about people and about myself. Most times, it is about friends in different situations who need to apply some wisdom or prayer in order to allow something good to happen to them or to stop bad things from happening to them.

 A personal example is when a friend of mine, who is one of the wheels of my vehicle, which means one of my strong-four, had been praying for the salvation of his father for about 10 years. All through this time, his dad had not been attending church and my friend did not stop praying for his dad. Being the usual practice that my believing friends and I meet every week to discuss issues of life, our victories and challenges, he told us about this challenge of his. We prayed about it and upheld our friend in prayer.

Then, on Saturday night which was five days after we had met together, I had a sweet fellowship with the Holy Spirit, and then, I went to bed. I woke up the next morning and I started praising God as the first thing on that day, and then, while praising and worshiping God, the Lord reminded me of the dream He had shown me over-night.

In the dream, I saw my friend coming out of the church auditorium, and I saw him just at the entrance of the church, pointing to his dad that he had just got saved! My friend was smiling in this dream and he was wearing a face cap.

Someone could ask, how do you know it is not just a mere dream? It is hard to explain but one thing is that when it is a dream from God, you know that you know that you know, moreover, God would remind you even if you forget.

For example, He gave Nebuchadnezzar the dream twice, he gave Joseph the dream twice, He gave Daniel the same kind of dream twice, and so, he reminded me while I was worshipping. When God speaks, His words contain big chunks of faith that when it is a message from Him to you, you just have THIS CONFIDENCE that He is speaking to you.

Anyways, I picked up the phone, called my friend and told him about the dream and interpreted to him as to what I felt the Lord was saying which was: "his dad was going to get saved that Sunday if invited his dad to church".

In a nutshell, he invited his dad, his dad came to church, his dad got saved that same day, and I saw my friend pointing to his dad at the entrance of the church auditorium, wearing a face cap with that same beautiful smile on his face, HALLELUYAH!

This testimony should be enough encouragement for someone to pray for God to activate their spiritual eyes.

Talking about prayer, someone might ask, but I don't know how to pray or what to pray. Let us talk about prayer in the next chapter.

SMALL QUIZ
What do you think symbolizes prayer in your vehicle?

Your Prayers
VS
Vehicle Pedals & Steering

Psalm 100: 4 - 5
"Enter into His gates with Thanksgiving,
And into His courts with praise,
Be thankful to Him, and bless His name.
For the Lord is good,
His mercy is everlasting,
And His truth endures to all generation".

Prayer is simply communication with God. We are to approach God by thanking Him for all He has done for us and for who He is, and then we can make our requests known to Him.

Using the vehicle for example, when we are driving, we are simply putting to use the power that is released by the fuel of the vehicle to move us from where we are to where we wish to go.

Like the vehicle, we are simply putting to use the power in the word of God, to move us from where we are in life to where God wants us to be. As time passes by, we grow in our prayer life and before we know, we are already praying like Prophet

Elijah.

God said "Let there be light and there was light". The Holy Spirit worked on the word of God to create the light.

When we pray, we confess what God has already said, and the Holy Spirit works on those words to manifest them in our lives.

When we pray, we are to pray in faith and faith is the substance of things hoped for, the evidence of things yet unseen. Faith is a spiritual substance. It already exist in the spiritual, we are only trying to bring it into the physical. The word of God releases that substance or faith into our spirit. And then, we use our words to convert them from the spiritual into the physical.

Therefore, when you pray to win the lottery or have your enemy killed, it is like driving a vehicle which is limited to gear 5, and because of one reason or the other you decide to use gear 6. It does not work because there is no gear 6 in that vehicle. You can only believe for what God has already provided and behold, He said He has given us all things that pertain to life and godliness! If your prayer pertains to life and godliness, you can believe God for it.

The pedals of the vehicle, when used with the gears, release the power of the engine to the vehicle. The navigation system directs, the driver presses the accelerator, turns the steering, applies the brake, flash the lights and move the wheels e t c in other to get to specific locations in life.

In essence, this is an active process. You have to decide to press the accelerator, brakes, clutches and turn the steering. You don't see a house in front of you and crash into it without pressing the brake. If your vehicle is moving towards a mountain, and you can see that a crash is about to happen, you would try to maneuver and turn away from the danger, and in the worst scenario, if the vehicle refuses to turn away from crashing into the mountain like in the movies, you would probably jump out of the vehicle to keep yourself safe.

Yet, in our walk of faith, people drive their vehicles of faith carelessly crashing into all sorts of barricades and mountains e.g. sickness, poverty, pornography, lust, drug, addiction e t c and instead of applying the pedals and steering of prayer coupled with the gears of faith, they just sit down in the vehicle, and allow it to crash again and again. They go about in bandages of shame, fractures of lack, testimonies of defeat, not knowing that in prayers, all things are possible.

Hosea 4:6
"My people are destroyed for lack of knowledge."

Brothers and sisters, without prayer, nothing happens. You can have all the fuel in the vehicle, you can have the most powerful engine, you can even start the engine, but only when you apply the gears of faith and press the pedals of prayer will the vehicle move.

Have you been stationary in your walk with God and you are wandering, why is this so?

How can a vehicle move without pressing the pedals? In order to progress spiritually with God, prayer is indispensable. Jesus Christ prayed every night, and He is the Son of God. If Jesus needed to pray, the question should not be when you pray but the question should be, when do you not pray!

Prayer is not primarily to make requests to God even though we can. More importantly, prayer should be the way we fellowship with God, the way we enjoy His presence.

Someone said, the baby believers always want God's **presents** while the mature believers want God's **presence**. It is alright to want God's presents because God's presents are really good and in fact, I like God's presents but brothers and sisters, we need to get to the place where God's presence is more fulfilling than His presents. That is called maturity.

Talking about prayer, prayer without praise and worship are dry and boring, and that is probably one of the reasons why God said, when we approach Him, we should approach Him with thanksgiving and praise. And if we want to praise God, we can as well praise Him very well.

Psalm 96: 1 - 4
Sing to the LORD a new song; sing to the LORD, all the earth. Sing to the LORD, praise his name; proclaim his salvation day after day. Declare his glory among the nations, his marvelous deeds among all peoples. For great is the LORD and most worthy of praise; he is to be feared above all gods.

SMALL QUIZ
What do you think symbolizes praise and worship in your vehicle?

Your Praise and Worship VS Vehicle Sound System

Psalm 150: 6
"Let everything that has breath praise the Lord. Praise the Lord!"

The sound system is one of the nicest things about a vehicle. These days we have mp3 players, cd players e t c that can easily be connected to the speaker of our vehicles, in order to make our presence in that vehicle more joyous and fun-filled. In fact, some people have video systems in their vehicles instead of just mere audio systems.

Now, when we drive, there are times when we are just in a hurry to get to where we are going, so that we don't even care about playing our sound systems. Those moments do occur but they are rare and should be exceptional.

Under normal circumstances, we start the vehicle, put on the seat belt, fix the mirrors and check the fuel level and other readings. Then we enter our destination into the navigation system and finally we play some really nice tune to make our journey as pleasant as possible. In fact, there are people who cannot do without a sound system in their vehicle.

So also as believers, while in that vehicle of faith, passing through the highways of life, we should endeavor to accompany this journey with a sweet smelling aroma of praise and worship.

Philippians 4: 4 - 7
"Rejoice, and I say again, rejoice.
Do not be anxious for anything, but in all things, make your requests known to God, with thanksgiving, and the peace of God that passes understanding with guard your hearts."

Apostle Paul makes it clear that when we make our requests known to God through prayer, we should do it with thanksgiving.

I strongly believe that praise and thanksgiving are the spices and seasonings that make our prayers taste so sweet to the Lord. In fact, we can take examples from Jesus Christ who from time to time thanked God first, before making His requests known. In fact, when He was asked by His disciples to teach them how to pray, He stated the following:

Our Father, who hath in Heaven,
Hallowed Be Thy Name --> (THIS IS PRAISE AND WORSHIP).

The kind of music that you play in your vehicle has the potential to affect your mood. Some music make you feel happy while some make your feel sad. In fact if you are the super-sensitive type, some music can make you cry. But, when we praise God and give thanksgiving unto Him, joy flows from the river of life in our hearts, burdens get lifted from our shoulders, chains get broken, we get strengthened, we feel strengthened and we are strengthened. A scripture just flashed into my mind right now which goes thus:

Philippians 4:13
I can do all things through Christ, who strengthens me.

Through the anointing of the Holy Spirit which begins to flow when we praise God, we start to feel that surely, we can do all things.

There is an example in the bible of a prophet called Elisha, who was asked to speak to God on behalf of two Kings. He didn't just start his vehicle of faith and drive down to the throne of God! What he did was that he asked for a harp player to be brought before him, to sing praises to God, and while the praise was going on, Prophet Elisha ignited his vehicle of faith, and within seconds, he was at the throne of God, and yes, God gave a word!

Now that is a man of God that understood the place of worship and praise, in his walk with God!

I implore you to study various men of God who allowed praise and worship to play a significant part in their walk with God. Shall we talk of David who made men and women worship God 24/7, or shall we talk of king Jehoshaphat, who made women who were singing praises to God to face a mighty army from 3 different countries, or Peter who praised God in a prison and an earthquake erupted and he was set free, or Joshua and the Israelites who praised God and the walls of Jericho fell down gallantly, or Paul, or the priests in the temple built by Solomon e t c

Brothers and sisters, I implore you to add the spices of praise to your daily devotion to God, and behold as the walls of your life begin to fall before you.

The psalmist says only the dead do not praise God. Does your finance or marriage or health or mood e t c appear dead, praise the Lord and see them raised back to life like Lazarus!

Your Ministry
VS
Vehicle Passengers

Exodus 19:4

'You yourselves have seen what I did to Egypt, and how <u>I carried you on eagles' wings</u> and brought you to myself.'

Exodus 32:9 - 10

"I have seen these people," the LORD said to Moses, "and they are a stiff-necked people. Now leave me alone so that my anger may burn against them and that I may destroy them. Then I will make you into a great nation."

The scriptures above show the great influence that Moses had on the destiny of the children of Israel. Here, they had boarded their vehicle of faith, which is called the Eagles' wings, and Moses-with a mind that commendably agrees with what God says- was the driver of the vehicle that was to carry the Israelites from Egypt to their destination, which was the Promised Land.

Now it happened that the children of Israel had grieved God, and because of this, God was willing to destroy them all but Moses pleaded with God and God heeded.

The passengers in your vehicle are the people that are entrusted to you spiritually. They are the ones that rely on you for nutrition, direction and correction. They are your families, friends, relatives, congregation, work colleagues etc.

So, what happens if you miss it as the leader? The analogy of the vehicle makes this very easy to understand. As the driver of a vehicle, the life of the passengers is technically in your hands. In fact, wherever you go, they go. If you miss it, they miss it, if you get it, they get it as well.

More importantly, the passengers of a vehicle can all get drunk with wine and it is not very serious because they will get over it, and still be alive. But if the driver of the vehicle gets drunk, and still retains his or her position as the driver, disastrous consequences are likely to occur.

A story of this kind occurred in the bible about David, who being the king of Israel became tipsy with a wine of pride when he decided to count the number of men in Israel. David at that moment felt he should measure and trust in his military strength rather than trusting in the strength of the Lord. The result was catastrophic not to David alone, but also to the people he was entrusted with.

Also, Jesus Christ being the spiritual head of the church is responsible for our destiny. He died and we died, He conquered the grave and we conquered the grave, He rose from the death and we rose from the death, He ascended and sat at the right hand of God and we did as well, He is the righteousness of God and we are the righteousness of God as well. This sounds really good!

Whatever Jesus did, I have the potential to do also, because I am in the same vehicle of faith with Him. He is the captain of our salvation. He is the author and finisher of our faith. He is the driver of our vehicle because we personally invited Him into our hearts as our Lord and Savior.

Now, please see something with your spiritual eyes.

Jesus is the head of the church and the church is the body. If you as a person eat a takeaway, you eat it through your mouth, which is part of your head, and then, your legs and hands and throat and fingers and toes e t c have also all eaten the same takeaway, because the food is transported to them individually by the blood in your veins. When God gave Jesus all power and authority, the same power and authority flows to us through the Holy Spirit.

Power is not lacking in the body of Christ, what is lacking are vessels that allow the power to flow. Set yourself apart to the Holy Spirit and see the power flow. That is maturity.

Once you are a believer, you own it a responsibility to cover your family, friends, relatives e t c spiritually. You are to feed them with the word of God, direct them with the word of God and correct them with the word of God as the book of Timothy states:

2 Timothy 3:16-18
"All Scripture is given by inspiration of God, and is profitable for doctrine, for reproof, for correction, for instruction in righteousness, that the man of God may be complete, thoroughly equipped for every good work."

It is good when the driver of a vehicle knows the way to a destination and better still, when the driver is in a sound state of mind. But how much better it is when all the passengers of the vehicle know how to drive the vehicle as well. In essence, the main driver can have a rest and someone else can take charge. In fact Moses expressed the same desire in the scripture below:

Numbers 11:29
Then Moses said to him, "Are you zealous for my sake? Oh, that all the Lord's people were prophets and that the Lord would put His Spirit upon them!"

I look forward to the day when the whole members of the body of Christ have reached such maturity, that anybody from the congregation can teach from the pulpit and preach the gospel with miracles, signs and wonders following. On that day, the devil would confess:
"Woe unto me, for the kingdom of God has fully come to the earth! "

Brothers and Sisters, let us drive ourselves into spiritual maturity!

Talking about ministering in power and authority, every seasoned minister of the gospel of Christ knows that fasting increases the amount of God's power that flows to and through them. Therefore, let's talk about fasting in the next chapter.

SMALL QUIZ
What do you think fasting represents in your vehicle?

Your Fasting
VS
Vehicle Servicing

Daniel 10: 2 - 5
"In those days I, Daniel was mourning three full weeks. I ate no plesant food, no meat or wine came into my mouth, nor did I anoint myself at all, till three whole weeks were fulfilled. Now on the 24th day of the first month, as I was by the great river, the Tigris, I lifted my eyes and looked, and behold, a certain man clothed in linen, whose waist was girded with gold of Uphaz!"

Luke 5:35
"But the days will come when the bridegroom will be taken away from them; and then they will fast in those days".

I personally do not like going hungry because it is not a very good feeling. But, I must say, I love what fasting does to me, it sharpens my sensitivity to the voice of God, it makes the power of God flow through me more easily and powerfully, it weakens my fleshly desires and strengthens my spiritual desires, it takes me closer to where God wants me to be.

Like the same reasons why we service our vehicles, it is to ensure that we get the best from our vehicles. For example, if vehicle A takes in 10 liters of petrol and travels 50 Miles, while vehicle B takes in 10 liters of petrol and travels 100 Miles, if the two vehicles travelled under the same conditions, then, I would prefer to have vehicle B. It is simple to see that vehicle B is more efficient and even cheaper to run!

Fasting would allow you to get much faster results than if you were to be praying without fasting. In fact, some prayers will not be answered unless you fast!

Matthew 17:21
"However, this kind does not go out except by prayer and fasting".

Like servicing a vehicle, the whole vehicle is checked for any damages and faults that might not be easily noticed. The engine is checked for wear and tear, engine oil is changed for easy flow of power, nuts and bolts are checked to make sure that they are not too loose or too tight, lubrication is applied where applicable to ensure easy flow of power, brakes, batteries, wipers e t c are all checked and at the end of the day, the vehicle would seem almost brand new again.

Fasting would allow you to check yourself with what God says in the bible, so that you can be a vessel that allows the power of God to flow to you and through you without hindrance. There is always power available from God by Jesus Christ through the Holy Spirit to us, but we must live in a way that allows that power to be able to flow to us and through us.

Matthew 5:8
"Blessed are the pure in heart, for they shall see God."

I personally believe that anybody can fast if they practice it regularly. Every time you plan to fast, pray that God would empower you to go through it easily. Fasting should become a habit and the only way something becomes a habit is when we do it consistently.

Ask a child who still crawls if walking is easy!

That child would tell you that walking is not easy. That child would complain about how the whole body is too heavy to be carried by just two tiny little feet. The child would go on to say that carrying the whole heavy body is achievable but moving the whole body while standing on two tiny little feet is a really big achievement.

Also, the child would say, if you wish to walk rather than crawl, it really depends on how long you want to walk for. If you plan to walk for 1 minute, that is alright because you can easily go back to rest on your knees. If you plan to walk for 5 minutes, then for security reasons, just make sure you have two bottles of energy drink by your side, because you would need it when you are done. But, if you plan to walk for 10 minutes or more, then, you must have written your Will!

Yet, under normal circumstances, we all normally walk for hours at a stretch sometimes without even thinking about it. That is the power of consistency. The more you do it, the easier it becomes and the better you become. Practice fasting one day every week and before you know it, you would be able to fast yourself into any victory!

A scripture flashed into my mind which I had never thought had anything to do with fasting, but after meditating on it, the revelation behind the scripture was unfolded. It goes thus:

Hebrews 12: 12 - 17
Therefore strengthen the hands which hang down, and the feeble knees, and make straight paths for your feet, so that what is lame may not be dislocated, but rather healed.

Pursue peace with all people, and holiness, without which no one can see the Lord: looking carefully lest anyone fall short of the grace of God; lest any root of bitterness springing up cause trouble, and by this many become defiled; lest there be any fornicator or profane person like Esau, who for one morsel of food sold his birth-right.

For you know that afterward, when he wanted to inherit the blessing, he was rejected, for he found no place for repentance though he sought it diligently with tears.

Please let us gently analyze this scripture through our spiritual eyes.

Therefore strengthen the hands which hang down,
Hands here indicate worship to me. Have you been worshipping without your hands raised up to the heavens? If your answer is yes then you might need to fast yourself into freedom in worship.

...and the feeble knees,
Knees here indicate prayer to me. Has your prayer life run dry and weak or you do not even have a prayer life at all? Do you notice that your prayers do not release power like they used to? If your answer is yes, then you need to fast.

...and make straight paths for your feet, so that what is lame may not be dislocated, but rather healed.

Feet here indicate your walk in life, your progress, your advancement. Your word is a lamp unto my feet, and a light to my path. Are there lame situations in your life? Are those situations getting dislocated or worse? If yes, then healing will approach you speedily as you fast.

Pursue peace with all people,

People might not really be the reason why we lack peace, we are sometimes the reason. Fasting would allow us to see the light.

...and holiness, without which no one can see the Lord;

Fasting allows us to check ourselves on the scale of holiness. And when we get to the place of purity in our hearts, God begins to show up in all the areas of our lives. We begin to see God.

...looking carefully lest anyone fall short of the grace of God;

Fasting makes us watch ourselves deeply. When we have successfully checked ourselves, then we can look out for others. We first check the speck in our eyes before pointing at the speck in another person's eye.

...lest any root of bitterness springing up cause trouble, and by this many become defiled;

Fasting allows us to see clearly if we are walking in bitterness or unforgiveness e t c which are major hindrances to prayers.

... lest there be any fornicator or profane person like Esau, who for one morsel of food sold his birth-right.

Fasting allows us to have self-control and also know the will of

God for our lives so that we do not miss God's plan for us.

For you know that afterward, when he wanted to inherit the blessing, he was rejected,

Fasting allows us to have a clear revelation of our inheritance in the Lord, and also to be spiritually mature to obtain it.

...for he found no place for repentance though he sought it diligently with tears.

Fasting allows us to know what we need to make repentance for in our lives, so that we can progress in whatever God has called us into, without having to go through the pain that comes with unrepentance.

Brothers and sisters, Jesus said that the time will come when they will fast, and now is the time to fast, now is the time to pray, now is the time to study your bible, now is the time to meditate on the word of God, now is the time to drive yourself into maturity!

Spiritual Highways
VS
Vehicle Highways

Matthew 7:14

But small is the gate and narrow the road that leads to life, and only a few find it.

A lot has been talked about already, from the body of the vehicle representing your body, to the engine of the vehicle representing your spiritual heart, to the driver behind the steering representing your mind or mindset or way of thinking, to the battery of the vehicle representing the brain of the driver, to the four wheels of your vehicle representing your friends of believers or strong-4, to the navigation system representing a function of the Holy Spirit, to the fueling of your vehicle representing studying your bible and the things of God, to the steering and pedals of your vehicle representing your prayer life, to the gears of your vehicle representing your faith, to the sound system of your vehicle representing praise and worship, to the passengers of your vehicle representing your ministry, to the servicing of your vehicle representing your fasting and finally, let us drive the vehicle !

Like a vehicle on the highway, there are rules that you work with in order to arrive safely at your destination. When the traffic light flashes red, you stop, if it flashes green, you move. You also need to have a driver's license, have a vehicle insurance in some countries, understand traffic signs e t c

Likewise, when driving your vehicle of faith on the spiritual highways or the highways of life, you need to be aware of a few things.

(1) Who are you in Christ?

You are a descendant of Father Abraham, you are born-again, you have been redeemed, you are an ambassador of Christ, you are a child of God, you have an heavenly passport, you are an alien in the world, you are loved, you are the righteousness of Christ, you are favored and blessed, you are the apple of God's eye e t c Allow the Holy spirit to minister these truths to you in your quiet times in His presence.

(2) What are your rights in Christ?

He became poor so that you can be rich, He redeemed you from the curse so that the blessings of father Abraham can be yours, by His stripes you were healed, you are joint heirs of the world with Jesus e t c

(3) What do you do if your right is being denied?

 You need to know how to flash your heavenly diplomatic passport on the highway of life. When sickness or poverty or shame or fear or discouragement or weakness or troubles e t c try to deny you the right that you have in Christ Jesus, demanding that you pay them taxes or fines or charges, you need to let them know that you have spiritual immunity.

Psalm 91:7
"A thousand may fall at your side, And 10,000 at your right hand, but it shall not come near you"

Do you know that diplomats cannot be charged on foreign soil? It is a known fact that sometimes you have to fight for your rights. That is why you need to know how to fight for your rights in the spiritual court of Law. So, what if sickness tries to rob you of your health, what if a demonic spirit of pornography tries to rob you of your fellowship with the Lord, what if the spirit of poverty tries to hinder you from reaching the poor, what do you do?

You take them to the court of God in prayer !

But before going to the court, you need to know who your lawyer is. You need to know what He charges for His service. You need to know if He has ever lost a case. You need to know His name. May I let you know that His name is Jesus? He is the greatest Lawyer ever. He has never lost a case. The last time that I heard, He won His case against death, poverty, disease, sickness, fear and every evil thing. He is our everlasting High Priest and He is the wisdom of God, no situation or circumstance can out-smart Him or over-power Him. And freely He gives us His service. Present your case continually through Him to God and prepare for a triumph.

2 Corinthians 2:14
"Now thanks be to God who always leads us in triumph in Christ, and through us diffuses the fragrance of His knowledge in every place."

Spiritual Thieves
VS
Vehicle Thieves

Genesis 4:6

So the Lord said to Cain, "And why has your countenance fallen? If you do well, will you not be accepted? And if you not do well, sin lies at the door. And its desire is for you, but you should rule over it. "

Revelation 3:20

Behold, I stand at the door and knock. If anyone hears My voice and opens the door, I will come in to him and dine with him, and he with Me.

When thieves notice that they can't rob you while you are driving your vehicle on the highway because you are the type that resist them, they would try to rob you when you park your vehicle!

A little joke that I used to play on my brothers' friends when they came visiting us was that, while the visiting friend is in the house in the company of my brother(s), with his vehicle parked outside the house, I would gently walk inside the house and ask him the following question:

"How much is the guy that is fixing your vehicle wheels charging you to fix them?"

Obviously he has not asked anyone to fix his vehicle wheels because they probably have no problems, so he would quickly rush outside to see if someone is trying to rob him of his vehicle wheels! It was usually funny to see them act with such fear! Obviously, I was not yet a born-again believer then!

Normal access to a vehicle is gained through a key. You open your vehicle and close it with your key. You start the engine of the vehicle with your key, and if you lose your key, you can hardly drive your vehicle. Now, if a thief has a duplicate of your vehicle key or perhaps, if they can break into your vehicle, there are high chances that your vehicle would be stolen or at least plundered. If you see a man creeping beside the door of your vehicle, playing around with the driver's seat window, that should raise an alarm. Yet, some believers have spiritual thieves around the windows of their lives and they don't even take notice or raise an alarm!

Spiritually, a key is vital information. When Jesus said to His disciples and to us even today: "I have given you the keys of the kingdom of God..." He did not hand over to them a metallic tool! He gave them information!

Genesis 4:6 says that if you do not do well, sin lies at the door.

The intention of sin is not to simply sit down at the door of your heart or at the door of your life, it intends to break in, sit as a passenger and if possible, take over the driver's sit of your life. Sin wants to rob you till there is nothing left for you to live on or live for, and then rob you of your life. Sin oversees a lot of evil spirits who drive men and women to do destructive things.

Think about it, the times when we operate in wrath, selfishness, revenge, wild partying, gluttony, hate, sex before or outside marriage, drugs, sexual perversions e t c we usually notice that there is a spiritual power behind it. As someone who gets angry so easily said to me once "If I don't release the evil outburst, it would be boiling inside of me!"

These are evil spirits who remove you from the driver's seat of the vehicle of your life, **for a moment in time**, in order to perform their evil deeds through your body or life! People give it different names namely: "When I am angry, I become a different person! I don't know where that came from!! I did not know what I was saying!!! ". **Of course you don't know because it was not you.**

Please recognize that sin is a spiritual force and not just some bad habits.

Romans 5: 21
So as sin reigned in death, even so grace might reign through righteousness to eternal life through Jesus Christ our Lord.

Grace is the spiritual empowerment that allows a believer to live in righteousness. It is the power that completely conquers the spiritual force of sin. Ethics cannot conquer sin, mere moral teachings in schools cannot conquer sin, willpower cannot conquer sin, self-improvement cannot conquer sin etc. Grace alone totally conquers sin completely.

Now grace comes through Jesus Christ and when He knocks the

door of our hearts, and when we let Him in, He conquers sin for us in those areas of our lives where we are willing.

John 10:10
The thief does not come except to steal, and to kill, and to destroy. I have come that they may have life, and that they may have it more abundantly.

There are spiritual thieves who are recklessly trying to break into the vehicle of your life! Vehicle thieves steal items that are usually easily replaceable, but these spiritual thieves want to steal from you, to kill you and therefore destroy you! They want to steal your joy, prosperity, health, purpose, children, blessings, fruitfulness, dominion, power, marriage e t c and finally your life!

They want to gain access either directly into your vehicle or life, or perhaps indirectly through thoughts that they trigger through words or ideas or suggestions. These spiritual thieves place their thoughts or ideas into your mind through people who yield to them in all areas of lives e.g. schools, religions, news, media, internet, friends, doctors, bankers, professionals, governments e t c

Now, let us look at what Jesus said in John 10:10
"The thief does not come except to steal, and to kill, and to destroy. I have come that they may have life, and that they may have it more abundantly."

What is life without good health? What is life without joy? What is life when you can't pay your bills or you can't even send your kids to the school that you know is good for them? What is life if you only make a living at the expense of spending time with your family? What is life if you lose your loved ones to sickness and diseases? What is life if you are bed-ridden and can't enjoy life? What is the essence of life if you are stuck to a wheel chair and can't even have freedom?

God created us to enjoy life and Jesus came so that we may enjoy life even more abundantly! He said, **may.** The reason why He said may, is because it requires our will. You need to be willing to have life.

Isaiah 1:19
If you are willing and obedient, you will eat the good of the land.

You need to be both willing and obedient to enjoy this abundant life! And this might sound shocking but it is true that a born-again believer is poor and sick and discouraged e t c only because he or she is unwilling. Because they are unwilling or lazy to study the word of God in order to renew their mind. Some Christians are obedient but unwilling, while some are willing but disobedient, but we have to be willing and obedient, the two conditions must be fulfilled to enjoy the abundant life.

Then He said: **"and that they may have it more abundantly."**

What is abundant life? Many of us have not even tasted life to its fullest and so, abundant life is inconceivable to us. The bible says look to Abraham your father, and to the rock from which you were taken from. Jesus lived abundantly. From the day He was born, He was blessed by wise men. Book of proverbs says that with wisdom are riches and honor. Jesus was blessed richly by those wise men. Yet Jesus' greatest riches is His direct relationship to God. When He needed to feed more than 5,000 people, the money was available to feed them but there were no bread and fish readily available in the desert and then, He tapped into His riches in the Father and just like that, His needs were met . Jesus was so blessed that Pilate the governor desired to see Him face to face!

Father Abraham was so blessed that king Abimelech recognized his presence in the community. Solomon was so blessed that the queen of Sheba sought to hear what he had to say.

Does your community or country feel your presence? Does your prime minister or king or president desire to hear what you have to say? When the world sees the abundance of your riches, wisdom, health, joy, honor, accomplishments, the world would seek you to teach them! That is abundant life!

If you need more examples in order to understand the life of abundance, find a tree that is bearing fruits! Find a mango tree, cherry tree, orange tree e t c and meditate on their abundance. If those are not easy to find, meditate on the abundance of the stars of the sky or the sands by the ocean.

When Jesus says **"I knock at the door,"** do not think He was talking to unbelievers. In fact, that verse is from His letter to the Lukewarm church in the book of revelation chapter 3. He is saying, you call me Lord, but there are areas in your life where you have not allowed me to Lord over. There are areas in your life where my instructions in the bible do not line up with what you do. He is saying to renew your mind so that your deeds can be renewed so that you can be like Jesus. He is saying, I have given you the power to overcome sin, which is grace, and with grace you can overcome. It is by grace through faith that we win in life.

1 John 5:4

"For whatever is born of God overcomes the world. And this is the victory that has overcome the world—our faith."

The kingdom of the world is a system that is driven by evil ideas or thoughts that come from the kingdom of the devil or darkness. Men and women from the past, starting from Adam and Eve, who to this very moment, yield to the ideas of the devil and sowed and are still sowing weeds, whose fruits we see in the world that we live in presently. The wars and diseases and sickness and poverty and selfishness and rebellion and murders and pride and confusion and greed e t c are fruits of the weeds sown in the past. For some of us, those weeds were sown in our lives before we became born-again. Now that we are born-again, we have to come against those worldly fruits in our lives by the spiritual power of grace.

By sowing the seeds of the word of God in our hearts, and not the same old same weeds of the world, we enter a cycle of godly harvests, and we begin to bear godly fruits of love, joy, prosperity, self-control e t c all of these in abundance.

The world knows that love solves all problems, but how can the world bear a godly fruit of love? You cannot sow greed and reap love. The love from the world is always a camouflage of self-interest as they say "there is nothing like a free lunch". But I tell you, in the kingdom of God, there is more than a free lunch! Jesus gave more than 5,000 people a free lunch with no strings attached.

The kingdom of the world presents weeds of ideas and calls them seeds. The kingdom of God presents the seeds of the word of God.

Choose between life and death but I implore you to choose life. Abraham chose life, Isaac chose life, Jacob chose life, brothers and sisters, choose life.

Your life is simply the fruits that abound based on what has been sown in your life, either by you or someone else. The earth only produces what is sown in it. We are like a spiritual earth. Therefore, we simply bear fruits that are spiritually sown in us.

Please recognize, if we refuse to till the ground, weeds automatically start to grow. When we are laid back from sowing the seeds of God's word in our hearts, we would simply notice the weeds of vices, cravings, lust, addictions, failure, disease, hate, e t c begin to grow in our lives. At this stage, we need to quickly take the weeds out and start tilling our heart and then start sowing continuously and daily.

We need to till our hearts and sow the seeds of the word of God to produce godly fruits. The word of God would soften the soil of our hearts and sow godly seeds in our hearts which would manifest in our lives as fruits of victory and life, if we keep our confessions in line with the word of God, but it takes time and effort from our side.

Therefore, if you have things creeping at the door of your life or perhaps they seem to be taking over your life, things like drug-addiction, sexual perversions, sickness of all kinds, diseases, unhappiness, discouragement, stress, medically unexplainable sicknesses e t c just allow Jesus to be Lord in that area of your life and receive freedom. Re-new your mind by continuously studying the word of God and thinking the way Jesus says to think, acting the way Jesus says to act, talking the way He says to talk, and see heaven back you up. See for yourself as the thieves around your vehicle get arrested by the angels of heaven, and you will experience the freedom and life that Jesus promised, even life in abundance.

So, what is the key to your victory in every area of your life? What is the key that keeps sin locked outside and keeps righteousness locked inside the vehicle of your faith walk?

Replace every idea in your mind with the word of God. Replace your mind with the mind of God. The bible reflects the mind of God. Why is David called a man after God's heart? David diligently observed what God says is right and wrong, and David replaced them with his own right and wrong. What a privilege, that we can have the same mind that God has! Therefore, think about what the bible says to think about, do what the bible says to do, and see the results that the bible says you will get.

For example, let's assume your doctor says you have cancer. The bible says you were healed by the stripes of Jesus. The doctor only says what he knows based on all he knows, which is very small. The earth is very small compared to the whole universe which is estimated to be billions of billions of stars. Man is very small in number compared to all the living and non-living things on the earth. There are medical experts in human bones, brain, eyes, teeth, muscles, hair, blood, skin, kidney, lungs e t c therefore, a medical doctor only knows a very small part of all that can be known about the human body.

Therefore and truly, your doctor knows something, but it is almost nothing. But, God knows all things, created all things and keeps all things!

Kindly keep it simple and just believe what God says in the bible. Also, confess what God says about you because your words carry the power to make things happen. Re-new your mind daily and continuously by studying the bible and I guarantee you, your blessing would come like the morning dew.

Like we have vehicle alarms that are triggered to make noise every time someone tries to break into our vehicles, we need to set our spiritual alarms also.

If something is in your life and the bible says it should not be there, let your spiritual alarm ring! If the pastor of a church preaches some message that does not line up with the bible, let your spiritual alarm ring!! If the doctor says something that does not agree with the bible, let your spiritual alarm ring!!!

Some people might say: **"mr Author, are you now saying that you have reached maturity yourself? "**
I say: **"kindly permit me to answer you with the scripture below:"**

Philippians 3:13-14

Brothers and sisters, I do not consider myself yet to have taken hold of it. But one thing I do: Forgetting what is behind and straining toward what is ahead, I press on toward the goal to win the prize for which God has called me heavenward in Christ Jesus.

I beseech you reader, pursue maturity and let your life preach the gospel without the need to speak a word, even as you await the coming back of our Lord Jesus Christ, who would reward you for your efforts according to His riches in glory, Amen.

Salvation Prayer

Dear God in heaven, I come to you in the name of Jesus. I acknowledge to You that I am a sinner, and I am sorry for my sins and the life that I have lived; I need your forgiveness.

I believe that your only begotten Son Jesus Christ shed His precious blood on the cross at Calvary and died for my sins, and I am now willing to turn from my sins.

You said in Your Holy Word at **Romans 10:9** that if we confess with our mouth the Lord Jesus and believe in our hearts that God has raised Jesus from the dead, we shall be saved.

With my heart, I believe that God raised Jesus from the dead. This very moment, I accept Jesus Christ as my own personal Lord and Savior and I declare that I am now saved and I am now a child of God.

Thank you Jesus for paying for my sins.

Dear Reader, if you said the above prayer with sincerity of heart, then, you are now a child of God. Congratulations. Start attending a bible-believing church, start studying the bible and start manifesting the kingdom of God on the earth.

Printed in Poland
by Amazon Fulfillment
Poland Sp. z o.o., Wrocław